The Selling Fox

A Field Guide for Dynamic Sales Performance

Jim Holden

John Wiley & Sons, Inc.

This publication is designed to provide accurate and authoritative information in regard to the subject matter covered. It is sold with the understanding that the publisher is not engaged in rendering professional services. If professional or advice or other expert assistance is required, the services of a competent professional person should be sought.

ISBN: 0-471-06180-8

Printed in the United States of America.

10 9 8 7 6 5 4 3 2 1

By wisdom a house is built, and through understanding it is established; through knowledge its rooms are filled with rare and beautiful treasures.

Proverbs 24: 3–4

This book is dedicated to my wife and lifelong friend, Chris Holden.

Acknowledgments

As solitary an effort as writing a book is, requiring weeks upon weeks of isolation and focus, in many respects it is a team effort.

Chris Holden, my wife and unfailing supporter in life, has really made this book possible. She has taken on many additional responsibilities, in both our private and professional lives, to allow me that quiet time, and also to assist me with this work—including countless "after hours" of editorial and personal support and counsel. If there is one person to credit for this book, it is Chris, for it absolutely would not be a reality without her, and it is with love and gratitude that I dedicate it to her.

Carol Jose, a long-time friend and writing colleague, also provided a great deal of support. Her editing ability and willingness to dive into new endeavors and topics was a tremendous help, as it has been on my previous books.

A special thanks is due to all of the staff at Holden International, for they personify the company's values of quality, innovation, and integrity. Each in his or her own way has provided inspiration to me in writing this book.

Contents

List of Figures and Tables   xv

Introduction   1

Chapter 1   **Closing Techniques**   5

Mastering the Basics   5
The Close   6
The Indirect Strategy: A Key Strategy to Master   15
Making the Customer Commitment Stick   18
Closing Like a Selling Fox   21
Selling Fox Talk   22
The Fox Ethos   22

Chapter 2   **Closing Dynamics**   24

Mechanics of a Trial Close   24
Close Condition Requirements   25
The Fox Ethos   34

Chapter 3   **Blocking and Trapping**   35

Blocking   35
Trapping the Competition   41
Selling Fox Talk   50
The Fox Ethos   51

Chapter 4   **Selling at the Edge**   52

Acknowledging the Possibility of Losing   52
Loss Recovery Plans and Techniques   53
Ranking Your Performance   58
The Fox Ethos   67

Chapter 5   **Calling High**   68

Executive Relationship Principles   68
Creating Balanced Value   76

The Seven-Step Executive Calling Process   88
The Selling Fox's Perspective on Calling High   98
The Fox Ethos   99

Chapter 6   The King of Sales Strategy   100
How You Sell Is Important   100
Indirect Is King   101
Real-Life Examples of the Indirect Strategy   109
Indirect Wins for Selling Foxes   118
The Fox Ethos   118

Chapter 7   De-Installing a Competitor   119
De-Installing a Competitor in a Major Account   119
A Fox-Like Approach to Loss Recovery   141
The Fox Ethos   143

Chapter 8   Qualifying Opportunities   144
The Opportunity Evaluator   144
Major Opportunity Evaluator   145
Major Opportunity Evaluator Summary   173
Short Cycle Opportunity Evaluator   177
The Fox Ethos   182

Chapter 9   Are You a Selling Fox?   183
Expanding Your Self-Performance Rating   183
Are You a Selling Fox?   187
The Fox Ethos   192

Chapter 10   Building Your Personal Business Development System   193
The Missing System   193
Design an Effective System   194
Applying Planning to Your System   196
Assessing Your Personal Capacity   200
Build Your Personal Business Development System   203
The Mark of a Selling Fox   210
The Selling Fox Ethos   211

Appendix: Portrait of a Selling Fox   212

Index   217

About the Author   221

List of Figures and Tables

Table 2.1	Timing the Close	26
Table 2.2	Sample Engagement Plan	32
Table 4.1	Loss Recovery Timing	56
Table 4.2	Loss Recovery Process	58
Table 4.3	Self-Performance Rating	63
Table 4.4	Example Self-Performance Rating	64
Table 5.1	The Fox Evaluator	75
Table 5.2	The Contact Evaluator	80
Figure 5.1	Creating Balanced Value	83
Figure 5.2	Balance Assessment Sales Tools	83
Table 5.3	The Currency Tabulator	84
Figure 5.3	Customer Impact Continuum	88
Figure 5.4	Support Base Map	94
Figure 5.5	Support Base Map with Key Players	95
Table 5.4	Competitive Contact Evaluator	96
Table 6.1	Indirect Strategy Matrix	104
Table 6.2	The Indirect Nature of a Fox	108
Table 7.1	Account Terrain Map	123
Table 7.2	Territorial Business Impact Map	124
Table 7.3	Potential Business Impact of Pursuing a New "A" Account	126
Table 8.1	Major Opportunity Evaluator I: Can We Add Value? Metrics Chart	146
Table 8.2	Major Opportunity Evaluator II: Should We Pursue? Metrics Chart	152
Table 8.3	Major Opportunity Evaluator III: Can We Compete? Metrics Chart	160
Table 8.4	Major Opportunity Evaluator IV: Are We Aligned to Win? Metrics Chart	167
Table 8.5	Major Opportunity Evaluator Results I & II: Business Value	174
Table 8.6	Major Opportunity Evaluator Results III & IV: Competitive Strength	175
Table 8.7	Prioritizing Opportunities	177
Table 8.8	Short Cycle Opportunity Evaluator I Chart	179

Table 8.9   Short Cycle Opportunity Evaluator II: Should We Pursue?
                 Metrics Chart   180
Table 8.10   Short Cycle Opportunity Evaluator III: Can We Win?
                 Metrics Chart   181
Table 9.1   Expanded Self-Performance Rating Chart   187
Table 9.2   Are *You* a Fox? The Selling Fox Evaluator   189
Table 10.1   Business Development Model   199
Figure 10.1 Account Profile Worksheet   201

Introduction

Every profession, every area of personal endeavor, has its aspiring new-comers and seasoned professionals. It may be in business, sports, the arts, or any area of life in which you find the full range of performers and their abilities. This book is about strengthening your personal perfor-mance in the area of professional sales in order to reach a quintessential level—that of a Selling Fox.

In every arena of selling, the focus is on competition—on facing that competition and winning. You may be selling solutions, commodities, or services. It doesn't matter. If you believe that the real differentiating fac-tor to your success is not *what* you are selling, but rather *how* you are sell-ing, then you're in the game as a Selling Fox plays it. You are the one to whom this book will speak most eloquently.

For years, I have written about and taught the concept of the Cus-tomer Fox, which is key to

- Protecting and growing important accounts
- Winning competitive deals
- Creating demand to produce new deals

Not necessarily at the top of an organization, a Customer Fox

- Shapes and personifies his or her company's operating values, setting high standards for integrity, quality, and innovation
- Works behind the scenes, allowing others to receive credit in those areas of the business in which he or she has little formal authority but wields significant influence
- Possesses a strong sense of mission or professional purpose, which is always aligned with the good of the company
- Is closely networked with others that make up his or her Power Base®[1],

---

[1]Power Base is a registered trademark of Holden International.

1

an influential body that de facto runs a company or division of a company in many of its aspects of operation

A company may have a number of Foxes who are the major forces within their organization, setting its strategic direction and operating philosophy while shaping corporate initiatives. Foxes are into all that will constitute their company's future. In many respects, these people *are* a company's future, but they are not alone.

Another type of Fox has emerged. Born not of operations, finance, or senior management, this new breed faces direct opposition every day of the week. They work in a world of constant uncertainty, depending on relatively little formal authority, living or dying by their personal skills, knowledge, and influence. Their companies and their customers support and depend on them, while competitors fear them. These are the rare breed of ultra high-performing salespeople—the Selling Foxes.

My professional life has essentially been dedicated to identifying and developing Selling Foxes. In my estimation, one Selling Fox is worth a hundred salespeople, for Foxes are the conscious competents who lead the way for others. They win deals while codifying their competitive processes and techniques to enable other salespeople to follow in their footsteps. Informally, they provide coaching and support behind the scenes, often without any additional compensation. They guide marketing and bring the voice of the customer into their company's corporate decision-making process, always working to align their company's interests with that of the customer base. Everything they do can be leveraged and tied to revenue generation, making them one of the most valuable corporate assets for a company in the new marketplace.

A Selling Fox is a Fox, and as such, is not well understood beyond his or her strong and consistent sales performance. Selling Foxes are not egocentric, not focused on themselves, but on their work and the results that it produces—you'll learn about how Foxes think and act in the Portrait of a Selling Fox provided in Appendix A. Therefore, it is not surprising that they are grossly unrecognized for who they really are and for the value that they truly represent to their companies.

The Selling Fox is intended to shine a light on these people and what they do, and is designed specifically to help you who aspire to become Selling Foxes. It is all about who they are, what they believe in as professionals, and specifically how they sell. It addresses what they do operationally to be so successful that they earn the recognition of being a Selling Fox. In that sense, this is very much a field guide that explores the route to the highest level of selling proficiency, which is where a Selling Fox operates.

As you read *The Selling Fox*, you will embark on a journey that begins with honing your closing techniques, striving to build strong operational proficiency to better manage peaking sales situations. Sales examples guide you through actual situations and customer dialog. The intent is to be explicitly clear as to how Selling Foxes use specific closing techniques to manage and win competitively sought-after orders.

Techniques on how to block and trap the competition, along with lessons in loss recovery, transition the focus from achieving high proficiency in the selling basics to mastering significantly more advanced selling skills. These are techniques that require not only skill, but also Fox-like cunning, as well as sensitivity to various timing considerations. Because these higher-order skills are challenging areas for most salespeople, the means and methods for self-assessment and continued self-development are presented as a road map to guide you in your journey to becoming a Selling Fox.

We highlight one of the most critical and least understood aspects of competitive selling—establishing and maintaining executive relationships. This section underscores the importance of knowing who you are as an individual, in addition to addressing

- The value that needs to be provided customers and the value that they need to provide to you
- Specific sales tools to assist you in calling high
- Specific processes to guide you in the use of these tools

Perhaps the second least understood aspect of engaging and defeating competition centers on strategic formulation. Chapter 6 describes "The King of Sales Strategy," the most effective approach to pulling the rug out from under the competition.

Selling Foxes know how to strike to win competitively held accounts. Chapter 7 explains how to de-install a competitor in a major account. In a slower economy, the only real way to grow market share is to take it away from the competition. In a faster, growing economy, the best way to destabilize competitors is to knock their cornerstone accounts out from under them; this is a topic that is addressed with surgical precision.

The focus broadens to address how to objectively evaluate large sales opportunities, smaller short cycle deals, large multinational accounts, and sales territories comprised of all types of customers. The effective management of such a diverse portfolio of accounts and sales opportunities is a key precursor to building your personal business development system.

Such a system is likely not yet included among the tools that your company will have provided you, but rather something for which you must look to a Selling Fox to learn. Foxes are the keepers of the guidance, structure, and wisdom necessary to master this most important aspect of your personal selling success. The map to building a personal business development system is provided in Chapter 10. Do well with this step and all the rest will fall into place.

We also offer you personal insight from Selling Foxes in well-known U.S. corporations, along with a chapter-to-chapter cataloging of Fox-like characteristics or attributes that define and shape how a Fox operates.

We think *The Selling Fox* will become the essential field guide for achieving sales excellence, with its very comprehensive table of contents for ease of use. It will direct you as you build your sales territory and accounts. Use it, excel, and become a Selling Fox.

1

Closing Techniques

Selling Foxes are unmistakable; they are distinctive not only in how they sell, but also in how they think. They reach a higher order of sales proficiency that requires across-the-board skills, from smooth execution of the basics to managing the most sophisticated aspects of competitive selling. Your success will ultimately depend upon your mastery of all the necessary selling skills, but that mastery will never happen if you don't learn to think like a Selling Fox.

Mastering the Basics

Let's begin with a refresher on the basics of competitive selling, recognizing that although they are referred to as *basic*, they are by no means simple to master. In fact, the basics are extremely challenging to implement well consistently. The key word here is *well*. For many experienced sales professionals, it is difficult to continue focusing on the basics. Sometimes the mindset is that experience takes them beyond that level because they believe that they mastered the basics long ago. It just doesn't fit their image of themselves.

However, a Selling Fox does not have these identity or perception problems. Nothing is beneath a true Selling Fox, or at too basic a level for him or her to address, whether it is consistently revisiting the basics of selling or examining how they treat people who are trying to be helpful in offering ideas or suggestions. Winning with an effortless style is what Selling Foxes do, but that doesn't happen without building wisdom in all areas of selling, including the basics in which strong tactical proficiency is very important. Selling Foxes recognize that wisdom has no boundaries, high or low.

The Close

Having said that, all basic competitive selling techniques are not created equal, and some are of far greater importance than others. For this reason, we begin with one of the most important aspects of selling—the close. Without a close, there is no customer commitment, and without a commitment, there is no sale.

What Is Closing?

Closing is securing a customer commitment—that is, reaching an agreement in principle that under certain conditions, the customer will purchase your solution, product, or service.

When Is the Best Time to Close?

You should close as early as possible, recognizing that if you attempt to close too early, it will simply serve as a trial close, which has the benefit of assisting you in learning very clearly where you are positioned in the competitive sales situation. A trial close also can identify obstacles that stand between you and securing an order or commitment.

How Do I Close a Sale?

First, recognize that there are three basic approaches to closing.

1. Soft close
2. Trial close
3. Hard close

The Soft Close: A *soft close* is nonconfrontational, never directly asking for an order. It is a common technique among salespeople, but Selling Foxes do not choose the common route, and they rarely opt for the soft close, as it can be indecisive and protract sales cycles.

The Trial Close: A *trial close* occurs when a closing is attempted and a conditional commitment is secured, or when the customer raises objections or additional needs that must be addressed in order to secure a close.

The Hard Close: A Selling Fox always goes with the more direct, harder style of closing, specifically asking for the customer's commitment. Recognize that at times, this will represent only an individual's personal commitment of support. It is not uncommon for a company to decide formally which supplier to choose in a closed-door meeting where no salespeople are present. In that situation, closing key people prior to such a meeting is critical. You may want to think of this as a type of trial close. In either case, a Selling Fox takes an approach that projects confidence and professionalism, while at the same time conveying sincerity. Too many salespeople lack this confidence and opt for the more comfortable and time-consuming approach of massaging the sales situation, never explicitly asking for an order. For some, it's insecurity that causes this; for others it is simply lack of skill.

To be a Selling Fox, you have to not only think like a Fox, but also act like one. You will develop your own way of closing, of asking for an order, but to give you a better feeling for the process, let's look at some role-playing or practice sessions that are Fox-like in nature.

🦊 Sales Example 1–The Pricing Objection

In this scenario, John is the key customer decision-maker. Mary is our company's salesperson. She has done a good job of understanding the customer's needs and has formulated a solution to addressing those needs, which she has just presented to the key people within the account. Mary is now ready to close—that is, to secure a firm commitment. After a bit of discussion, Mary makes her closing pitch:

> *"John, we have been working together for some time now to develop a solution that will address your company's needs, and I think that you agree that it is a reasonable approach. Given that, are you comfortable going with us?"*

> "I like your approach, Mary, but I am not prepared to make a commitment at this point."

"What do you feel still needs to be addressed, John? And how can I be helpful?"

"You have done a lot already, Mary, and we are very appreciative, but . . ."

Sales Analysis: Exposing an Objection

Mary is now at a classic point in the closing. An objection is about to surface. A Selling Fox will now listen very carefully to what the prospective buyer has to say. The good news is that Mary will be made aware of the buyer's problem and will take specific measures to handle the problem without losing focus on her objective—to close. Mary's Fox-like technique in responding will be to direct the subsequent dialogue and process in such a way that

- She understands precisely why she is getting a no or a delay from the prospective customer.
- She is able to deal with the negative issue immediately.
- She will make a trial close—that is, secure a conditional commitment.

Keep in mind that if Mary had not attempted to close early, she might never have known there was an issue still to be resolved before the order could be secured. She'd only know later that for some unexplained reason, she did not get the business. This brings us back to attitude. Objections are not bad, so avoid any urge to be defensive when they surface.

As a Selling Fox, you must always understand what you're dealing with before you can begin to manage it. More importantly, if you can anticipate issues or problems, you can prepare, and then nail them on the spot.

Continued Dialog

Let's return to the sales example dialog. John is speaking.

"You have done a lot already and we are appreciative, Mary, but the price is a definite problem. It is simply too high for us."

"John, I understand the need to be cost effective, but tell me, what specific problem does the price cause for you?"

"Well, it is a question of budget, Mary. When we decided to go forward with this, we budgeted what we thought was the right amount, but quite frankly, we did not consider all that would be involved. There is just no way that I can go back to my management and ask for more money for this."

"I understand that, John, but in demonstrating to your satisfaction that we can address the budget issue, perhaps through leasing, or maybe by downsizing the system configuration where we will address the most important aspects of the application in the short term, and then expand the approach as you go into your next fiscal year when new funds could be available, would you then be comfortable in going with us?"

Sales Analysis: Key Response Techniques–Identify, Probe, Jump

Mary employed three key sales techniques here: *identify*, *probe*, and *jump*.

1. She *identified* the objection without responding with emotion or argument.
2. She *probed* to elicit the true concern behind the objection. A Selling Fox never accepts an objection on face value.
3. She *jumped* by addressing the underlying concern only to the extent necessary to jump the objection.

The Fox-like jumping technique demonstrates that a credible approach exists to solving the customer's problem. What Mary did not do was specify exactly how she would solve the budget issue. Specifics would most likely require that she speak with other people within her company, thereby aborting her effort to close the deal. That kind of self-containment, when a sales situation is peaking and a decision is about to be made can be disastrous for the sales professional. When closing, always identify, probe, and then jump any objections.

John's response to Mary's alternative proposal takes the process a step further:

"Are you certain that we could address all of our A-list requirements in the short term, Mary? You know what we have to get done."

"I do, and I am also confident that we can demonstrate that understanding beyond any doubt, but I will need to move quickly to organize the revised approach and present it to you. On that basis, are you prepared to give me a green light?"

"Yes, but subject to our review of the revised proposal, of course. How long will it take to pull everything together?"

"Not even a day, John. We've done this before, and it has always gone very smoothly. Why don't we plan to meet again at this same time tomorrow?"

"Fine."

"John, is there anyone else who should be involved in that meeting?"

"No, I don't think so. I'll brief my boss later on the main points of our discussion. He might want to sit in tomorrow, but I doubt it."

"That's fine. He's certainly welcome to join us. I will call you later today to confirm, and look forward to seeing you tomorrow."

Sales Analysis: Benefits of a Trial Close

What can we learn from this situational dialog?

- We determined that the only issue between Mary and the order, from the customer's point of view, is budget.
- What we don't know is whether the origin of the budget issue resides with John or with his boss.

If it lies with John, and is under his authority, no problem. If it is with his boss, that could be a horse of a different color. John will have to go back to his boss and be just as convincing and logical as Mary was with him. He may or may not have that ability. Or he may be able, but not willing (perhaps even uncomfortable) to put the argument in front of his boss. In either case, we will need to get to John's boss to help him out. Sometimes the Johns of the world will ask for this help, but most often they do not. It is more common that they feel a sense of authority in making the decision, often saying, "I am the decision maker and there is no need for you to work with anyone else." This is very normal. John's manager wants him to take responsibility for the decision in order to engender personal commitment, but that does not mean that his boss will not influence John in subtle but important ways.

Let's look at how Mary specifically advanced her sales campaign:

- She accomplished a trial close, having secured a conditional commitment. It revealed not only the impending budget concern, but also the chain-of-command issue. She successfully jumped the budget problem and will now have to build substance to her approach in a revised proposal. The time for Mary to sort this out with the customer, however, is not now, but before she goes for the final close.
- She will now also be certain to meet with John's manager, with John's support, to ensure that the budget issue is effectively addressed and confirm that John can actually make a buy decision and commitment.

That's another reason that you can never close too early. Trial closes, professionally executed, will tell you whether a person does not have the authority to commit. Such discussions will often lead you to an accurate understanding of the approval process, indicating who has to sign off on the deal. It is your job to ferret out any concerns that people in the approval chain may have relative to your proposed solution, product, or service, clearing the path for a favorable decision.

Sales Example 2—The Surprise Negative Referral

This sale presents a rapidly developing, real-time problem for Mary, our sales professional, to solve.

Mary has been working with Bill, the decision-maker for a prospective customer, and it is going very well. She has strong competition, but is certain that she is in the lead as she approaches a point in the sales cycle at which she should be able to close. In fact, the customer recently requested the names of several referrals from her—a very positive sign.

Mary calls Bill to make an appointment to see him, ready to initiate the close.

"Good morning, Bill. How are you today?"

"Not very well, Mary. In fact, I am very upset."

"I'm sorry to hear that, Bill. I hope we've done nothing to upset you. What is the problem?"

"It's those referrals you provided. The first one I contacted told me that your company's support has been terrible and that you have not fulfilled any of your commitments the way they expected you to. They said that if they had it to do over, they would never buy from your company again. I can't tell you what a spot this puts me in, Mary. I have supported you and basically presold my management on going with you. Now, I feel like you've made me look like a fool. And I don't like looking like a fool to my management."

"Bill, needless to say, I am as surprised as you. Did you speak personally with Sally Smith, whose name we provided?"

"No, I didn't. She wasn't available. I ended up speaking with someone else who said he is familiar with the installation. Fred Mason is his name."

"I see. This is obviously very disturbing to me, and I assure you, I'll get to the bottom of it very quickly. While I do not have firsthand knowledge of any negative situation, I can tell you that what you were told by Fred is not indicative of us as a company. I am absolutely certain that if problems exist, they are being properly resolved. I'd like to follow up on this immediately and, in fact, would like to do so right now. This is in no way what you can expect from us. By the way, did you speak to any of the other references?"

"No, quite honestly, I was so surprised at that one, I made no other calls."

"I understand."

Sales Analysis: Response and Probing Techniques

Sound far-fetched? This actually happened to me early in my sales career. It taught me to be prepared for anything when a sales situation is peaking. If ever something is going to go wrong or the competition is going to launch an offensive, it will most likely be at that peak point. In this case, the customer was as surprised as Mary, the salesperson, to encounter a negative referral. But watch how Mary deals with it, again using the identify, probe, and jump techniques that we discussed earlier in sales example 1. When this referral was provided, Mary believed that it was a good one, reflecting a very successful installation; she therefore couldn't imagine what had gone wrong. First, note that even with little or no understanding of the situation, Mary, who is a Selling Fox, did not become defensive in responding to the customer's agitation and negative remarks.

 Any form of argumentative response is the kiss of death for a sale.

On the contrary, in situations like this, as a Selling Fox, you should articulate what you believe to be true, based upon all that you know about your company in terms of what it stands for as an organization. It is critical that you project confidence in your organization. Don't challenge, but don't be meekly accepting of such blatant criticism either. View it as an opportunity to meet the customer challenge with confidence and determination. Also, keep in mind that in situations like this, not only is the sale at risk, but your reputation and that of your company are on the line as well. Time is of the essence. You'll need to investigate quickly to ascertain the facts of the situation.

Having identified the problem, Mary begins probing, which will require several steps in order to understand exactly what is behind the situation.

The Process

The first thing Mary needs to uncover is:

- Who is Fred Mason?
- What is his position in that company and his authority level?
- Why was he so negative toward Mary's company?

After making a few quick phone calls, Mary determines that Fred is the buyer who supported Mary's competition when the purchase decision was being made to buy from Mary's company. Fred's preferred vendor was apparently overruled by his management. Therefore, he had an ax to grind.

The next fact-finding issue in the probing process is to determine whether there's any substance to Fred's charges that Mary's company has not done the job as promised.

Mary determines that the installation was successful and that her company's service and follow-up support have been very good. In fact, the customer is completely satisfied.

The third piece of information that Mary needs to learn is how Fred Mason came into the picture when Sally Smith was the reference given?

Mary calls Sally and learns from her that Fred just happened to receive the call from Bill and seized the opportunity to retaliate against Mary's company.

Now, having ascertained the pertinent facts, and spoken personally with her designated reference person, Sally Smith, Mary is ready to go back into the meeting with Bill and jump the objection by presenting her rebuttal:

"I have just spoken to several people involved, Bill, and now have an understanding of what happened. Fred Mason apparently had his own agenda in making those negative assessments, which have nothing to do with our true performance or us. In checking with his company, I've learned that his comments to you were out of line with the reality of the situation. That installation and my company's support have been very good. I apologize that you were unduly alarmed. Sally Smith, whom we referenced originally, is the person actually in charge of our installation and she'll be calling you later today and will attest to its unqualified success. It is unfortunate that this occurred, but as I mentioned earlier, it is in no way indicative of what you can expect from us. Bill, in demonstrating to your satisfaction that we actually performed in a superior manner for this customer, in contrast to what you heard from Fred Mason, will you be prepared to go forward with us?"

Bill pauses a moment to think things over.

"If all is as you say, Mary, and providing the other referrals also check out, I don't see any problem."

Sales Analysis: Restoring Customer Confidence While Closing

Again, Mary jumped a very strong objection, addressing it only to the extent necessary to reestablish her company's positive image with the customer and secure a conditional commitment.

Sometimes this process goes smoothly, but other times when you are hit from left field with a serious negative situation, as Mary was here, it can be very challenging to stay focused on your objective—to close.

Keep in mind that other similar situations that can create just as much adverse impact as a negative referral are often created by the competition specifically to destabilize your sales effort and damage your credibility. Selling Foxes aren't drawn off base by such tactics. Changing the decision-making criteria in the eleventh hour of a competitive sales situation can be a powerful competitive move; this issue is addressed in more detail later.

The Indirect Strategy: A Key Strategy to Master

Consider this: You are in the final stages of a competitive sales situation and your competitor is stuck in second place, or so it appears. While not overconfident, you feel that you are going to win the business—it's in the high-probability column of your sales forecast.

Changing the Ground Rules

What may not be apparent to you at that point is that your competitor is setting the stage to introduce new issues to the sales situation that will influence the customer either to change the decision-making criteria or to alter the weighting of the criteria, propelling the competition into the lead. In effect, the competition is *changing the ground rules*, an important competitive sales strategy and technique.

The problem, assuming that you could effectively respond to such changes, is that you do not have enough time to respond. The strength of this sales strategy is in its stealthy nature.

Your competitor knows that in order to succeed, he or she must time the shift in decision-making criteria perfectly, just as the sales situation is peaking. If anything, the competitor will err on the late side, knowing that injecting new information into the customer buying process at the last minute will easily contain or slow down a customer's decision to go with you. That can conceivably happen even if the customer has indicated that yours is the solution, product, or service that his or her company prefers.

As a Selling Fox, you need to always be on the alert for new decision-making criteria that may originate in a department different from the one to whom you are selling, or that may come down from the customer's senior management. New criteria could come from anywhere you are not. The operative word above is *alert*. Most sales professionals tend to develop a false sense of security when they are clearly in the lead.

When a Selling Fox is about to pull the rug out from under a competitor, using an indirect sales strategy, which we have just illustrated in one example but discuss later in greater detail, the Selling Fox counts on that sales competitor being a bit overconfident. It contributes to the element of total surprise in the turn of events.

Note that the four basic sales strategies—direct, indirect, divisional, and containment, as well as how to identify a Power Base—are discussed in greater depth in my previous books, *Power Base Selling: Secrets of an Ivy League Street Fighter* (first published in 1990 and still in print) and *World Class Selling: The Crossroads of Customer, Sales, Marketing, and Technology* (1999), both published by Wiley.

Sales Example 3—Delivery and Missing Approver Objections

In this scenario, our Selling Fox Mary has been working the account for some time. Andrew is her key contact. Having just completed a compelling presentation on her company's solution to addressing the customer's needs, Mary is ready to close and is in a discussion with Andrew.

> "*As you can see, Andrew, we are well qualified to meet your needs. Having demonstrated that, are you prepared to make a decision?*"
>
> "I would like to, Mary, but we still have a few things to sort out."
>
> "*Well, we would certainly be pleased to assist you. What issues do you see?*"
>
> "I am concerned about the long lead time in terms of delivery. You

quoted six weeks and I understand why you cannot have the system shipped before that, but it creates problems for us. Our new product schedule has been accelerated and we will be in production three weeks earlier than planned if our estimates are correct. No way can we hold up production for that long."

"Nor would we want to create such a problem for you."

Mary pauses to think the matter through for a moment. She knows that she needs to be sensitive to the new requirement, but must also find a way to jump it. She then responds.

"I have several thoughts on this, Andrew. How would you feel about our providing an interim system and support, on a loaner basis, to accommodate your immediate production needs? While there are of course some details to work out, I am absolutely confident that we can address your near-term production concerns, so that the delivery date of the system won't impact your production schedule. In demonstrating that to your satisfaction, recognizing that there is more detail to be covered, would you be comfortable making the decision to go with us?"

"That sounds good, and I would like to give you the green light, Mary, but we are not prepared to make a decision on this today."

Mary probes. *"Are there other concerns I'm not aware of, Andrew?"*

"I know that you realize that this is a very important decision for us and that a lot is at stake. For that reason, this acquisition has strong visibility within our organization. As you know, Mary, my department has responsibility for this decision, but what you may not be aware of is that one of our senior vice presidents has pronounced views about which company we select. Unfortunately, she is out of town this week or I would introduce you to her."

"I understand, and can appreciate your need to cover all the bases, Andrew. If your V.P. is supportive to our approach, and please be assured we will assist you with whatever you need in presenting this to her, even to bringing in our own senior management to do that—if, again, she is supportive, will you then go with us?"

"I will meet with her early next week to brief her on your suggestion. If that goes well, we will have a deal. Can you hold our delivery slot until then and still be able to firm up whatever is necessary on the loaner system?"

"Yes, I'm sure we'll be able to handle this in a way that will adequately accommodate your scheduling needs, Andrew. I will get back to you later today to address the details of the loaner."

At that point Mary shakes Andrew's hand and begins to talk about implementation details to help cement the conditional commitment.

Sales Analysis: Jumping Multiple Obstacles to Close

In this sales situation, Mary encountered two obstacles that were in her path to a successful close, and using the identify, probe, and jump technique with each, succeeded in jumping both. In some cases, you may encounter even more—or you may discover that the ones that surface are considerably more difficult than these two were.

Nevertheless, the Selling Fox's reaction remains essentially the same—identify: surface the issue or objection; probe: get to the underlying concern and evaluate it; and then address the problem to the extent necessary to jump over the obstacle.

This last closing scenario reveals that Mary had done a good job but had missed a key step in the competitive selling process: getting to and understanding the senior executive's involvement in the sales situation.

Don't Skip Steps!

Selling is a step-by-step process, and if you skip steps, you will have to go back and make them up, often with very little time to do so. On that note, one more step is required after the senior executive gives her support to Mary: She must solidify the close by making the customer's commitment virtually nonretractable.

Making the Customer Commitment Stick

Once you've succeeded in securing a customer's commitment, conditional or otherwise, you as a Selling Fox know that the next step is to take precautions against the competition's attempts to turn the order around. This is especially critical during the time between when you receive a verbal "yes" from the customer and the time you receive a written commitment or order.

Advertising and Trapping Techniques

Solidifying a purchase commitment involves two sales techniques that are the mark of a Selling Fox: advertising and trapping.

- **Advertising**—Immediately after you have secured a final commitment, get to other people in the account and casually or informally advise them that a decision has been made in your favor. Time is of the essence in doing this! The more people who know about the decision, the better. It is not uncommon for key decision-makers to question or doubt their decisions after the fact. There is also the potential impact of a competitor's well-planned loss recovery effort. As a Selling Fox, you know you must do what it takes to make it awkward for the key decision-makers to reverse their decisions—or worse, suddenly switch over to your competition.

  Recently, I read a newspaper article announcing "Harris wins Army deal worth $287 million." It appears from the article that the win on the deal by a division of Florida-based Harris Corporation was leaked to the press even before the final contract was issued—a quintessential form of advertising. While such a tactic often may not be advisable, no one wants to appear indecisive. But that is what will happen if key decision-makers have indicated internally that you are the chosen vendor or partner of choice, and then reverse that position. Of course, customer senior management could get involved and reverse the decision, which brings us to a second competitive postselling technique.

- **Trapping**—A Selling Fox anticipates that as soon as the competition hears that they have lost the order, they will attempt to jump over the heads of the customer people who support the winner in an effort to turn the order around. This type of end run, so to speak, is very common; knowing how to trap the competition and secure the order is essential. Informally, you advise your contacts who support you that while it would be clearly unethical and improper, their credibility and decision-making authority might possibly be challenged by the competition. You must make it clear that you and your company would never engage in such negative tactics against a competitor, and that you hope that your competitors would not either, but that it could happen. The point here is to connect a possible competitive end run with the fact that should a competitor succeed in getting senior management to countermand the decision, that would call into question your key contact's decision-making ability and authority. It might become company rumor that this was a decision turned around by higher management—a tremendous negative reflection on the key decision-makers involved and specifically on their judgment. You must present this idea in such a way that your supporters will view such an action by a competitor for what it is—a negative attack on their credibility as decision-makers in the company.

Sales Example 4–Trapping to the Competitive End Run

Our salesperson Mary has just secured a commitment. She is in the process of advertising it (spreading the word) by informally and casually making Stan, a key decision-maker, aware of what the competition might do. Mary and Stan are on the way to the coffee machine when Mary opens the dialog.

> *"Stan, I would like to take a moment here to share a concern with you. While I would certainly hope that this won't happen, it is possible that when the competition learns that they have not been selected, they may try to jump over your head and go to your manager, or even to his boss, to try getting the decision reversed."*

> "You have nothing to worry about on that score, Mary. My department has the authority on this."

> *"I know it may be hard to believe, as it would clearly send out the message that the wrong decision was made and that it needed to be reversed, but such negative tactics are not beyond the realm of possibility, Stan, believe me. The competition may simply refuse to acknowledge that authority."*

> "Do you think that's a possibility?"

"Yes, we have seen this tried before. At our company, tactics like that are forbidden. I could lose my job if I ever displayed such a lack of professionalism. Unfortunately, that is not the case in all companies. It simply indicates that some very competitive salespeople are willing to sacrifice the credibility of a person like you just to get an order. They don't care how bad it makes you look to your management; they just want the order."

"Now that you mention it, Mary, I guess I have seen it happen before, but let me be clear, it will not happen here. In fact, I am planning to speak to my manager today, and advise him that we've made a final decision on this order, which by the way, he is already somewhat aware of. That way, he'll know what's been done, in case anything like that is tried on us. I may even let him know of your concern."

"That's a wise move, Stan. You know better than anyone how hard we have all worked to make this project a success."

"I sure do. No kidding, Mary, if they try something like that, I'll see to it that they are shown the door."

The trap has been set.

Trapping is a very valuable sales technique to master, as the Selling Fox knows. A clever counterthrust to a competitor's maneuvering or negative selling tactics, it is a customer education process that, when done skillfully and with Fox-like cunning, allows the competition to trap itself. The trapping technique is further explored in examples throughout the chapters ahead.

Closing Like a Selling Fox

When executing a trial close or trying to secure a final customer commitment, a Selling Fox always implements the following nine-step closing process, or a close approximation of it.

Closing Like a Selling Fox

1.   **Anticipate objections.** Ask yourself, "What could go wrong? Could the competition pull the rug out from under me?"

2.   **Close early.** Determine where you stand. Surface what is, or could be, an obstacle between you and an order.

3.   **Close hard.** Be explicit in asking for the business. Listen carefully to the customer's response.

4.   **Identify.** Surface all objections one at a time and stay focused.

5.   **Probe.** Don't focus on the objections; get to what is behind them.

6.   **Jump.** Address objections only to the extent necessary to jump over them.

7.   **Close explicitly.** Frame up a commitment, even if it is a conditional one.

8.   **Advertise the decision.** Let others know; lock down the commitment.

9.   **Trap the competition.** Anticipate a negative competitive response and set the stage for the competitors to trap themselves.

Selling Fox Talk

How you speak, the specific words you use, can be critical in executing sales basics that involve customer dialog, especially when closing. Let's revisit the operative phrases that can help you to construct or reinforce your communication skills and effectively implement the closing strategies discussed.

The Fox Ethos

This book is as much about who Selling Foxes are as it is about how they sell. At the end of each chapter, we revisit a number of Fox-like characteristics or attributes that will serve as a guide for you in building your own selling philosophy or ethos.

Selling Fox Talk

Opening the closing dialog: . . . *I believe that you would agree that we have a solid approach to addressing your needs . . .*

Opening to the jump: . . .*in demonstrating to your satisfaction . . .*

Projecting confidence: . . . *I am absolutely confident . . .*

Asking for the order: . . . *would you be comfortable in going with us . . .*

Demonstrating confidence in the absence of facts: . . . *this is in no way indicative of what you can expect from us as a company . . .*

Jumping the price objection: . . . *I am very sensitive to the value of money, but help me to understand the specific problem that our pricing causes for you . . .*

Opening to advertising: . . . *would it make sense to chat with some of the other people who will be involved in the project and let them know that we will be working together?*

Opening to the end run trap: . . . *now that you have made a decision, you might want to be prepared for any negative tactics that might occur . . .*

The Fox Ethos

Nothing is beneath true Selling Foxes, nor at too basic a level for them to address, whether it is consistently revisiting the basics of selling or examining how they treat people who are trying to be helpful in offering ideas or suggestions.

Selling Foxes always go with the more direct, harder style of closing, specifically asking for the customer's commitment. They do not shy away from difficulty.

Selling Foxes take an approach that projects confidence and professionalism while at the same time conveying sincerity.

Foxes are rarely argumentative and always proactive in their selling techniques.

2

Closing Dynamics

In Chapter 1 we talked about how a Selling Fox addresses the issue of closing in terms of professional selling. We looked at the trial close, which can surface obstacles that might remain between you and ultimately securing an order.

Mechanics of a Trial Close

Understanding the mechanics of a trial close leads us to other sales techniques that are the foundation of competitive selling, giving you the ability to create a virtual minefield for your competition. To illustrate, let's look at a sample early trial close dialog.

Sales Example 5—The Early Trial Close

Mary, our Selling Fox, queries George, the decision-maker, about the status of his company's evaluation process. It is early in the sales cycle; nevertheless, Mary does a trial close. Her objective is to uncover any information she can that might be pertinent to the sales campaign.

> *"George, I know that it is still early in your evaluation process, but if you were to make a decision today, how would we fare?"*

> "It is difficult to say, Mary, because as you know we have just sent out the request for proposal. But based on what I know about your offering and your company, I would say that you are in a very competitive position."

"Thanks. We want to stay on top of this. I understand that Bill, who heads manufacturing, will be approving any decision that is made, as the equipment will be going into the production area. Any sense on how he might view us?"

"Well, you are right—Bill is certainly a key player in this. I think he has worked with your company in the past. I don't recall exactly when."

Sales Analysis: Trial Closes Uncover Important Information

Mary confirms that Bill will definitely influence the decision-making process, and she learns something new: he has apparently been a customer of Mary's company before. This is the point of a trial close—to uncover new information that might present an advantage or an obstacle to obtaining an order. Therefore, it is appropriate to use the trial close on a frequent and continuing basis.

In our example, you see that Mary prefaced the dialog by saying, "I know that it is still early in your evaluation process." This statement gave her license to shift into an exploratory mode in which George would be comfortable, knowing that Mary was not actually asking for a commitment.

Close Condition Requirements

So when can you ask for a commitment? You will continue to be in a trial close mode when any of the following three conditions are not present in the customer:

- Readiness
- Willingness
- Ability

The requirements that produce a close condition and their relationship to the buying process are shown in Table 2.1.

As you can see, the issue of determining when you can close is one of recognizing close condition requirements and their relationship to the customer individuals involved. This underscores the need to understand and (to the extent possible) manage the approval process, which

Table 2.1 **Timing the Close**

Close Condition Requirements	Buying Process
Readiness	Decision-making
Willingness	Approval
Ability	Funding

is when you are most exposed to competitive threat. A Selling Fox pays close attention to all three phases of the customer's acquisition process but pays particularly close attention to the approval phase, as it can informally become part of the decision-making process.

Readiness

Customers will not be ready to make a commitment to any supplier if they have not yet evaluated all available options. This means that decision-making criteria have been identified and the process for evaluating companies against those criteria is in place. Generally speaking, the process consists of a formal evaluation followed by the necessary management approvals to proceed. We refer to these two steps as the *decision-making process* and the *approval process*.

It is easy for salespeople to never really understand these two distinct and separate processes when competing for business. A Selling Fox, on the other hand, not only carefully maps out both processes, but continuously checks for changes, as a Selling Fox knows that one sure way to lose business is through the last-minute involvement of new customer executives in the approval process. That can not only catch you off guard, but can also make it difficult to know who is actually the source of any new objections that might surface. You can end up defeated by a phantom influence—one you hadn't identified. A Selling Fox knows that the best protection against that problem is to never stray far from the decision-makers and approvers, constantly monitoring who is or who could become involved in the buying process.

Only when the customer has evaluated all the appropriate suppliers as part of the decision-making process has the readiness state been satisfied, but readiness alone is not enough to support a "buy" decision. The customer then moves on to the willingness phase of the purchasing cycle.

Willingness

Typically, the decision-making process brings the customer down to a short list of suppliers that they have determined qualify for the business. This means that when viewed against the decision-making criteria, several companies likely will make the final cut. Often, it is the product of the willingness state that narrows the field to one preferred supplier. You want to be that preferred supplier, so this state should be monitored with diligence. Willingness centers on the perception of the key decision makers (i.e., the managers of the decision-making process) as to how the approvers, the people that make up the approval process, will feel about the various companies that have made the short list. Very simply, the decision makers often reason that if the approvers are supportive of a particular company and they recommend that company to the approvers, it will be a positive reflection on their judgment. If the decision makers recommend someone else, they will know very quickly that they have erred because a series of questions will come flying back at them about justification for their recommendation. For this reason, it is not uncommon for an informal exchange or dialog between the decision-makers and approvers to take place throughout the evaluation process.

This is not to say that individuals who are evaluating suppliers should not speak their minds and recommend the companies they believe in, as many do. What it suggests is that many do not, and as salespeople, we need to be aware of that and be prepared to deal with it.

After a short list of companies has been identified, evaluated, and approved, the willingness state has been met.

After the readiness and willingness conditions exist, only one hurdle stands in the way of a commitment—the ability state.

Ability

Of the three acquisition states, this is the most objective, or mechanical, if you will. Simply put, in order for a purchase commitment to be made, the funding must be present to support the acquisition. While this sounds fundamental, it is not uncommon for salespeople to confuse a purchase decision with a purchase commitment.

For example, they learn that they are the supplier of choice and then wait endlessly for the order to appear. As long as the approvers have not signed off on the funding, the salesperson will have to continue to wait while in a very competitively vulnerable position. Vacations, business trips, and any number of unanticipated logistical issues can come into play, further holding up the receipt of the actual order.

For those reasons, a Selling Fox begins to focus his or her attention on the customer's funding process as early as possible in the sales cycle.

Adding all this up means that the buying process has four distinct phases that a Selling Fox will actively track to secure an order in the shortest amount of time possible, actively monitoring and managing:

- The decision-making process
- Decision-maker perceptions of the approval process
- The approval process
- The funding process

The operative words here are *monitoring* and *managing,* and the best way to accomplish them is by trial closing the customer on a consistent basis throughout the sales cycle. This does not mean trial closing the same person day after day, but rather broadening your exposure within the account by trial closing everyone who is appropriate, particularly the approvers, in order to understand and clarify:

- What they know about your company and offerings
- How they feel about you
- How you can better position yourself with them

Managing the Customer Buying Process

If you focus on three key elements in your sales campaign, you will maximize your ability to manage the buying process:

- The value that you can potentially provide to the customer
- The amount of risk and the manageability of that risk, which the customer will assume in working with you
- The cost of ownership to the customer in relation to the value you will provide and the risk that they will assume

These three elements will position your solution relative to the customer's needs, the buying process, and the competition.

How do I structure my approach to addressing a customer's needs in order to project maximum value to the customer, while also showing minimal risk and cost of ownership to them?

The answer to this question is very straightforward: develop a consultative, solution-oriented approach to addressing the customer's needs that enables you to build and communicate the following to the customer:

- Understanding
- Commitment
- Ability

Conveying Understanding

To maximize value and minimize risk to the customer, you need to deliver a very high-quality solution that addresses their needs. That begins with mutual understanding. Knowing the following, as a minimum, is required as a checklist:

- What they want and need to accomplish
- What is important in how they address those needs
- What they will expect of you as a supplier (or perhaps as a partner)

Also, recognize that not all their needs are equally important to them. Another issue further complicates matters—you will find that prioritizing those needs will often be a function of which person with whom you speak in the account.

The best way to build this mutual understanding is by asking questions—not just any questions, but the *right* questions. If your questions reflect insight and relevance to their needs, you will establish credibility and trust with the customer early on in the sales cycle. There is also no better way to broaden your exposure to their senior management than by showing how your insight into existing corporate initiatives connects in some positive way with the solution you plan to propose.

Although the questions will vary by sales opportunity, of course, the following list contains examples of some typical questions. They should assist you in formulating your own set of questions, consistent with your business and the types of customers who buy from you.

- "What are you (the customer) trying to accomplish, and why?"
- "How will you measure success?"
- "What business value will be created?"
- "Who is driving this within your organization?"
- "What kind of role do you see us playing?"
- "Are you open to suggestions that might be out of the box or non-traditional in nature?"
- "Are you familiar with our firm or with the work that we have done for other clients?"

The key is to understand that it is not what you say, but what you ask that will help you to develop the insight necessary to wage an effective and competitive sales campaign.

At this point in a sales cycle, a Selling Fox checks his or her products and ego at the door before entering the account.

It may be useful to create a context for this questioning process. When you first begin your meeting with a customer, you will go through the customary pleasantries. It's small talk, but it is important because you are getting to know each other. Next, you move into the business phase of the meeting, which should commence with your providing an introduction to your company. You then go on to present a very brief overview of how you feel that your firm can be of assistance to the customer. Again, keep it brief and then transition the lead to the customer, indicating your desire to better understand their business and needs. Ask the customer executives to provide you with an overview of their business; this information sets the stage for you to begin asking specific questions. Remember to listen carefully. Understand what is being said and communicate that understanding by appropriately restating key points. If you do not understand what the customer is saying, absolutely do not fake it—ask questions, even if it slows the discussion down a bit.

Demonstrating Commitment

Even with the very best understanding, if you and your company are not committed to the customer's needs and the customer's business success, the quality of your solution may be compromised, decreasing value and increasing risk to the customer. All salespeople say that they are committed, so how does a customer determine whether that commitment is real? How do you, as a salesperson, engender customer confidence in your level of commitment to them?

Customers who have worked with you in the past likely know that your word is dependable, but don't consider this to be a given. In today's world, many people are sincere only because they have to be, or will profit in some way by feigning sincerity, which means that they are not sincere at all. These are the same people who believe that they are telling the customer the truth or that they are not lying even though they conveniently omit important information. They inappropriately package or bias information, damaging the image of all professional salespeople. Therefore, as a Selling Fox knows, you need to establish and reestablish your integrity with each new account and with each new person in every existing account.

> *Absent any history, establishing integrity involves creating a tangible expression of your commitment.*

Formulate an Engagement Plan

Often, the biggest customer concern that you will face in relation to your proposed solution will be, "will it work for me and my needs, and how can I be certain that it will work that way?" Address this concern with real clarity and you will be well ahead of the game. The way to do that is with a plan like the following engagement plan in Table 2.2.

Your engagement plan should consist of a number of items that operationally map out what is required to ensure the success of an installation. They very clearly identify what will happen, why, when, and what

Table 2.2　**Sample Engagement Plan**

Item Number	Description of Action	Objective	Timing	Required of Customer
1	Application review meeting	Detail roles and responsibilities Set implementation schedule	June 15th	A purchase order Management participation
2	Software customization	Create a customer-specific solution	Completed by July 30th	Assistance in finalizing the design specification document by July 1st
3	Training of customer personnel	Transfer technology Provide for self-support	Completed by August 15th	Participation of all appropriate personnel Core team to be dedicated full time for 3 months
4	System installation	Increase manufacturing output by 30% within 6 months	August 30th	Completion of all preinstallation planning and preparation
5	Performance review	Assess impact Formulate recommendations for improvement	November 30th	Production line testing support
6	Executive briefing	Report project status and level of success	December 15th	Participation of senior management

the customer's responsibilities are in contributing to that success. This plan will establish you as a thought leader and make your commitment to addressing the customer's needs very tangible, thus enhancing your credibility in that company. It will also serve you well as an operational document, particularly as it relates to organizing your own internal resources. Additionally, it can shorten sales cycles by creating a sense of customer urgency after they have seen the plan. The sooner the customer places an order with you, the sooner you can get started on this obviously carefully thought-out solution to their needs. Many times, companies delay making the final purchase decision but hold your feet to the fire on delivery commitments. The engagement plan approach addresses that problem.

Showing Ability

You may have an excellent understanding of what is required to ensure the success of your solution and be very committed to achieving that success, but you and your company must have the ability to perform—that is, *functionality* if you're selling a product, or *expertise* if you are selling a service. It is the core source of the value that you will provide, often expressed as so-called features and benefits that many salespeople feel are at the top of the list when it comes to generating competitive advantage. Although they are certainly important, if you are selling solutions, features and benefits take a back seat to projecting understanding, commitment, and ability, which assure the customer that he or she will receive maximum value with minimum risk and minimal cost of ownership.

Demonstrating that you and your company have the necessary resources to do the job not only addresses the question of ability, but also enhances customer confidence in you. It becomes clear to the customer that you understand what is required to achieve success, and that your company is willing to dedicate the necessary resources to the project to ensure that success. The more specific you can be in identifying key resource requirements, the better. This higher level understanding of what is required to ensure a successful installation is the mark of a Selling Fox.

The Fox Ethos

Continuing our examination of who Foxes really are, let's look at two additional defining characteristics, seen within the context of competitive selling and specifically this chapter.

The Fox Ethos

At this point in a sales cycle, Selling Foxes check their products and ego at the door before entering the account. Selling Foxes put the spotlight on the customer, not themselves, or their products, or services—the customer is always center stage.

Absent any history, establishing integrity involves creating a tangible expression of your commitment. The integrity of Foxes is always evident in their work, which accelerates relationship building.

3

Blocking and Trapping

A s we have discussed, a close becomes a trial close when one or more of the readiness, willingness, or ability states is not present. At the same time, until you have a firm purchase order, you are vulnerable to being out-sold, which brings us to a competitive selling technique called *blocking*.

Blocking

There are various ways to use the competitive blocking technique. Here is one example:

Suppose you are in the 11th hour of a competitive sales situation in which a decision is about to be made and the customer has invited you in to give a final presentation.

First or Last In?

The quick response of most salespeople to this question is to be last in, for two good reasons:

- By being last in, you can often assume that the readiness, willingness, and ability states likely will be present, telling you that a hard close condition exists—you could leave that presentation with the order in hand.
- By being last in, you have an opportunity to challenge the previous competitors' approaches to addressing the customer's needs, without their necessarily having the ability to counter.

Being first in has pro and con considerations:

- Pro: It gives you the opportunity to trap the competition, a competitive selling technique that will come up throughout this book.
- Con: The downside of being first is that the hard close condition—all states are present for securing the order—probably will not exist. If you were to try to close as first in, the customer response probably would be, "Well, as you know, we do plan to make a decision this week, but we have not finished our review of each company's approach."

The disadvantage is that the readiness state is not present.

Even so, the preference of Selling Foxes is often to be first in, especially if they know that the presentations will take place over a period of time, so that they are better able to manage the decision-making process.

 To be last in is good, to be last-last in is best.

Here's why: You arrive at the customer meeting, you are first in, and present your approach, making sure that you convey understanding, commitment, and ability. At some point during the discussion, you refer to a key piece of information to be provided to the customer, that you don't have at that moment, but that you anticipate will legitimately be available to you only after the date of the last competitor's presentation. This may take some research or work on your part, but it can be done honestly.

Such key information may relate to delivery or to a new capability that your company will be introducing by that time. It may involve a call from your CEO to the customer's senior management that can't take place until a certain date, or any other piece of information that will be significant and relevant to addressing the customer's needs.

What you are doing here is controlling the timing of the information to remove the readiness state when your competitor(s) present their company's approach, in order to prevent the last-in competitor from closing the deal.

With the block in place, the stage is set for you to go back into the

account right behind the last competitor. You are now positioned as *last-last* in.

Blocking is a fairly straightforward competitive selling technique that is based on the timing of information. The challenge is not how or when to implement it, but rather how you think about a sales campaign.

What Is the True Purpose of a Customer Presentation?

Some would answer that it is intended to put forth your approach to addressing the customer's needs or to build credibility, especially if you are doing a demonstration. Others might say that it is to establish understanding, commitment, and ability. All these responses are true, but are not the only reasons for a customer presentation.

 *To a Selling Fox, the true purpose of a customer presentation or any other customer activity is to generate competitive advantage.*

That mind-set opens up your thinking to all the factors that could impact your competitive position—like who should attend, as well as the timing and content of the presentation. A salesperson who is not competitive will never attempt to block the competition when the opportunity arises.

Selling Foxes are always competitive; therefore, they always block when it makes sense to do so. Ask a Selling Fox why he or she lost an order and you will always hear, "I was outsold" or a similar response.

Only noncompetitive salespeople think that they have lost an order because the price was too high or because the product lacked functionality. Certainly there are exceptions, but generally speaking, if you lose a qualified sales opportunity, you were simply outsold. That mind-set will center your focus on determining how you were outsold and what you could have done differently. That is the first step in determining what you can do better in the future.

A Selling Fox would rather be a good learner than just a good performer any day of the week because a good learner ultimately becomes a great performer.

Dealing With Objections

When we discussed jumping customer objections in Chapter 1, we did so within the context of objections that surface during the closing phase of a sale. However, objections can surface at any time during a sales cycle; when they do, you need to be prepared to address them very effectively. To accomplish that we use a proven objection-handling process.

It all begins with a problem; remember, however, that many objections can exist in unspoken form, which is why it is so important to be trial closing whenever it is appropriate to do so. The sooner you surface a problem, the sooner you can identify it, probe it, and jump it. In other words, you have to expose the problem in order to deal with it.

As you will remember from Chapter 1, the first step in dealing with an objection is to listen. Let the customer describe the issue—you focus on what is being said. Ask questions to ensure your complete understanding, and to communicate that understanding to the customer, along with the fact that you personally care about the customer's concern and the issue raised. For many people, this comes naturally because they care and it shows, but for some it does not show even though they do care. It is important that you get credit for caring.

Part of building that understanding is to probe what lies beneath the objection. Perhaps the issue centers on the absence of specific functionality. After you understand what capability is missing, you need to determine how and why that creates a problem for the customer. It is not unusual to find that the problem is not relevant, but rather is a manifestation of the competition: they have a capability that you don't, and they have convinced the customer that it is critical to the success of the installation.

 Remember: having product benefits beyond that of the competition is only as good as they are significant to the customer.

Don't be surprised when such significance is competitively created.

Now, let's assume that the customer's problem has been identified and understood. The next step is to formulate an approach to addressing the problem, which becomes a project management challenge. It involves developing a strategy and aligning the necessary resources and people to get the job done, but keep in mind that the sales side of the equation remains. As the account executive, you have the responsibility to determine the source of the objection. If it is not the competition, ask yourself who within the customer's organization would be most concerned about the problem. Involving the right customer individuals in the process will:

- Ensure that the problem does not resurface later in the sales cycle.
- Broaden your support base in the customer's organization through good problem-solving techniques.

Think of dealing with objections as negotiating. It is easy to think of negotiating as that which occurs at the end of the sales cycle, finalizing price and terms of the sale, but the negotiating process actually begins the first moment that you meet with a customer. You negotiate to influence the decision-making criteria, trying to encourage the customer to put more emphasis on criteria that align with your offering's strengths. When you respond to a request for proposal (RFP), you are negotiating. When you attempt to involve higher-level customer executives in the sales cycle, you are negotiating. When the customer asks when you want to schedule your presentation, you are negotiating. There just isn't any time during the sales cycle when you are not negotiating in one form or another.

This particular aspect of selling can be very challenging. Most negotiating courses are intended for people who are purchasing; only a modified version of that course is generally offered for sales professionals. Often such an offering will not work well because the techniques used in procurement generally do not transfer easily to sales. One aspect of negotiating that does carry over, however, is managing the attitudinal aspect of a negotiation.

Sales Example 7–Negotiating Customer Objections

A well-known example of negotiating is that of a person's wanting to purchase a house. The asking price is $200,000. What if, without any hesitation, the buyer makes an offer to purchase the home for $180,000? Then the seller immediately accepts that offer. How do you think they both will feel? We'd say, "Uncomfortable." Why? The seller is probably thinking, "If I had been a bit more patient, perhaps I could have gotten more for the house, something closer to the asking price." At the same time, the buyer might be thinking, "Hmmm. They accepted my first offer right away. Did I pay too much? Could I have bought it for less?"

The Attitudinal Aspects of Negotiation

The attitudinal aspect of negotiating is very real. If people do not feel right about a negotiation—that is, if their emotional needs are not met by the negotiation process—the deal may not stick because one of the parties could look for ways to get out of it.

The same is true when you are managing objections or any other aspect of the selling process. Customers must feel that they have been heard, that their business is important to you, and that you are sincere in your motivations.

If you use the following negotiating style in the objection handling process, coupled with good attitude management, you will find that it can be adapted to all forms of customer situations. It is a process that uses the same three steps, but differs from that of handling objections during the close in that it is more detailed. Earlier in the sales cycle, you will have time to do more of an in-depth analysis of the issues. Often you can actually solve the customer problem through negotiation to overcome the objection rather than jumping it in order to secure the conditional buy commitment, as you would do later in the sales cycle. Let's walk through the process:

- *First, identify.* Listen carefully and build a solid understanding of the issue. Ask questions and demonstrate your understanding while projecting your real concern for the customer. It is imperative that your motivation be to do the right thing for the right reason, and not just to get an order. Make that mistake and the attitudinal aspect of the process will work against you, sometimes creating just the incremental advantage that the competition needs.
- *Second, probe.* Get to the underlying concerns and determine where within the customer's organization they originate. Be particularly sensitive to competitively installed concerns.

- *Third, solve.* Shift into a project management mode. Formulate a solution and mobilize the necessary resources to implement it in a timely manner. This will neutralize the objection and build your reputation for producing results. Every time you implement this process within an account you will precondition people to be more receptive to you next time around. In fact, it can get to a point with a particular customer that when you acknowledge a new concern, you have so much credibility that the customer takes your word that it will be satisfactorily addressed, thereby de-emphasizing it as a problem. That is the space where a Selling Fox lives.

Trapping the Competition

In selling, professionalism and process are supreme, but even with the best of process and the most sincere level of professionalism, not all objections can be effectively addressed as we would like. Some are more problematic than others because the competition may have an overwhelming advantage over you in specific areas.

At that point, you will rely not on your ability to address the objection to succeed, but rather on the competitor's lack of professionalism and their predictability. It is an advanced technique that can become a defining moment in a sales campaign, creating a decisive win for you.

Sales Example 8—Trapping to Negative Selling

Let's assume that the competition has functionality or specific capabilities that your product is lacking. Perhaps in six months or so your research and development (R&D) people will catch up, but for now it is a big problem. Bolstered by a sense of overconfidence, the competition has engaged in negative selling against you. They have been making it very clear to every customer manager involved that your product is inferior to theirs, in the most graphic and specific terms possible. How do you deal with this tactic? In my experience, there is only one way. It's not surefire, but often it is very effective.

The process begins with good intelligence as to what exactly the competition is saying. Assume that they are mudslinging, attacking your product and saying that it cannot do three things that theirs can. Let's say A, B, and C represent these competitive capabilities. Assume also that your company's R&D group is aware of your lack of capability and is working to correct it. In fact, your company is very close to introducing new functionality. As a Selling Fox, you have significant influence within your company, including the R&D group. Using that influence, you request that the new capability not be immediately announced to the marketplace at large, but instead be phased into the marketplace in order to maximize competitive advantage. Here's why:

As you begin working with a potential new customer, you take the time to discuss your personal selling philosophy—not over a conference table, but on the way to the water cooler, at lunch, or some other informal setting. You explain that like his or her own organization, yours is a very professional company, and that there are certain activities in which they will never catch you engaging, like negative selling. You explain what that means and how your focus is consistently on the customers, their needs, and on your company's producing the very best solution to addressing those needs.

The dialog between Richard, the customer, and Mary, your company's sales executive, might go something like this.

"Richard, because we are new to working with each other, I would like to take a moment to share with you our company philosophy in building a new customer relationship. It's pretty simple really, but not one shared by all companies. We put a heavy emphasis on professionalism, which means that you will never catch me disparaging the competition. That kind of negative selling is off-limits in our company. You know, things like focusing your attention away from your needs and requirements and onto competitors' deficiencies, as if you as a manager could not do an evaluation of the various companies for yourself."

"Well, Mary, I hadn't really given any thought to it, to be honest. I'm more concerned with equipment performance and our needs at the moment. Why do you see this as such an important issue?"

"I raise it for a very good reason, Richard. It has been our experience that companies who engage in negative selling tactics also tend to bend the truth. They misrepresent the facts and often have something to hide about their own

performance, which is why they are focusing on the competition. You will find us to be very straightforward. We will always level with you about what we can and cannot do."

Sales Analysis: Educating the Customer about Professionalism

Do you see the messages that Mary is conveying to the customer in this dialog? She is basically educating the customer about the value of dealing with a more professional organization. This message needs to be repeated and reinforced with a number of customer individuals who appear to be of high integrity and have a role to play in the buying process. Remember that you are trapping to the blatant disparagement of another company by the competition. Also keep in mind that as you set a trap, you are educating the customer and can sometimes walk a fine line between that and being too negative about your competition—don't cross that line.

But the trap is not yet set. One more ingredient is required—the fix, so to speak. You know that the competition is stronger than your company in several product capability areas, but what the competition does not know is that in one of those areas, your capability has improved. It may not be great, but it is not bad either. You communicate your solution, including the new fix to the customer, being very honest about what you can and cannot do, but at the same time emphasizing your new capability.

The hope is that the competition will come in and do as they have in the past. Then it happens. Your competitor dives into a negative selling mode, detailing to the customer all that is wrong with your product, including that you lack capability in the area that you have been stressing to the customer, the one in which you have new capability. On a good day, that discussion between Richard and your competitor might look like this.

♦ Sales Example 9—The Trap Snaps on Negative Selling

"Richard, I hope that you are not considering XYZ. Their product is woefully deficient in many areas, particularly A, B, and C. There is no way that they can do the job," says your competitor.

"I'm not so sure of that," Richard responds.

"Well, we compete against them all the time and I can tell you that they are using old technology. When it comes down to A, B, and C, they just don't have it."

"I disagree. In fact, I just saw a demonstration of their capability in the C area. It looked pretty good."

"Well, are you sure about that, Richard? To my knowledge, they don't have C at all."

"I think that there may be a lot that you don't know, and furthermore, I am concerned about your lack of professionalism. Why all the negative selling? Why are you trying to shift my focus onto your competitor?"

"I wasn't trying to do that, Richard. I was just trying to help you with your overall evaluation."

"You don't think we are capable of doing our own evaluation?"

"No, of course you are, I didn't actually mean that."

"Then what did you mean?"

Sales Analysis: Competitors Trap Themselves

You can see how a conversation like this can go. Educating customers about what professionalism entails arms them with the ability to ask intelligent questions that can be very disorienting to the competitive salesperson. Many times the competitor will even become argumentative with the customer. In that way, they are actually trapping themselves, pulling the trigger on their own credibility. You simply set the stage by educating customer individuals who are receptive, as they possess a personal operating philosophy that reflects high integrity, will not tolerate being manipulated by an external influence, or want you to win the business.

Again, it is very important that you fully comprehend trapping as an *educational* process. Your job is to equip the customer with a streetwise understanding of what is actually taking place when a competitor engages in certain manipulative activities. It is not to directly advise the customer individual on how he or she should respond or react to the competitor. If you do, you will be telling the customer how to do his or her job, crossing the line that I mentioned earlier and potentially trapping yourself.

Because there is so much mudslinging in the marketplace, negative selling is a classic when it comes to trapping.

Competitive Price Slashing

Another arena for trapping is anticipating a significant last-minute drop in a competitor's price. In this situation, your competitor senses an imminent loss and attempts to buy the business. Sometimes when this happens, competitors are simply buying market share, but at other times they have no intention of actually securing the business. So why would they do it?

If competitors have concluded that they cannot win, they may feel that the next best thing is to drive up the cost for you—forcing you into a position in which you believe that in order to win the business, you need to discount your solution deeply and/or make major resource commitments that will all but destroy your margins. Thus, you need to be prepared for such tactics.

As with negative selling, trapping against significant discounting requires that you build a logical infrastructure to support your discussions with the customer. Let's go to an example dialog and then review the infrastructure upon which it is based.

Sales Example 10—Trapping to Price Discounting

The sales situation is going well, you are about to close, and you anticipate getting the order. Remember that this discussion is taking place in a very informal manner. You are the salesperson opening the conversation with John, the purchasing manager.

> *"John, we very much appreciate all the support that you've provided and we look forward to a very successful project. Does everything continue to look good on the budgeting?"*

"Yes, we have allocated the funds and don't anticipate any problems."

"You know, one thing that you might want to anticipate, and hopefully it won't happen, is a radical last-minute move on the part of our competition. Sounds strange, I know, but it happens. A company senses that it is not going to get the business and decides to drastically cut its price. The company's hope is to secure the business, but more importantly to create customer dependency on the company so that in the future it can find a way to recapture its lost margin. You're an experienced businessperson, John, and you know that if a product is properly priced, your supplier will have the margin needed to provide good service and support to you. If a company precipitously drops its price, it means that it has to be made up somewhere else, maybe by cutting back on service. If that is not the case, the product may just have been overpriced to begin with."

"Sounds manipulative. We certainly want a good price, but not at the expense of service during the installation or the ongoing support we'll require. This project needs adequate service to be successful. Price is important, of course, but we cannot compromise the success of the project."

"You're right, John, it is manipulative. Inexperienced customers might think that they are getting a great deal, but you're an experienced businessperson and you understand pricing. Sometimes a competitor will even jump over your head and go straight to senior management. They basically want to take control out of your hands. It is not professional, but it happens."

Sales Analysis: The Language Techniques of Trapping

Again, trapping is an educational process. You are causing the customer to think about an anticipated competitive action before it happens so that they can ask penetrating questions and see the competitor's action for what it really is: unprofessional and manipulative. In this example, and in the normal course of business, the points of logic in terms of operative phrases that make up its infrastructure are:

- *Drastically cut their price: Drastic* is the key word here, as we are talking about something out of the ordinary.

- *To create customer dependency:* Dependency implies that the customer will lose some measure of control.
- *Cutting back on service:* Cutting back establishes that a price must be paid; nothing is really free.
- *The product is just overpriced to begin with:* Overpriced explains how a company can afford to cut its prices drastically, again suggesting a manipulative aspect of how the competitor operates.
- *Sometimes a competitor will even jump over your head:* It is important to set your traps with as many people as possible. In this case the customer may well go to the manager and give him or her a heads up as to what could happen.
- *They basically want to take control out of your hands:* The customer does not ever want to lose control of his or her project. Warning the customer in this way thus reinforces the fact that a competitive price-drop attempt would be akin to a personal attack on the customer individual.
- *It is not professional, but it happens:* Not professional labels the competitor.

Again, it is this type of dialog, conducted informally and often with multiple customer individuals, that sets the stage for the competition to trap themselves.

Sales Example 11–The Trap Snaps on Price Discounting

Now let's look at how this conversation might actually take place when the unsuspecting competitor dramatically cuts the price.

> *"John, I know that you are very close to making a decision as to which company you will be working with on this project and I am very pleased to advise you of a shift in our pricing. Because you are a very important customer for us, we are prepared to reduce our price by nearly fifty percent if you will agree to go forward with us today."*

> "That is a very significant offer and it is certainly appreciated, but tell me, how can you do that?"

"Well, again, it is because our management recognizes your importance as a customer."

"I understand, but how will you maintain your margins? Is this going to cost me in reduced service or support?"

"Definitely not; we would never do that."

"Well then, how can you do this? I am just trying to understand how this works. I mean, was the product overpriced in the first place?"

"Definitely not; this arrangement is an exception to how we typically price our products."

"Well, if your other customers were to become aware of this, wouldn't they want similar discounts?"

"Yes, but they will never find out about it—we maintain confidentiality."

"Let me see if I understand this. You are willing to disadvantage your other customers, pricewise, for us. So if you will do that to them, how do I know that you will not in some way disadvantage me in the future?"

"Oh, we would never do that, John—your company is special to us."

"I think that I have heard enough. We appreciate your offer and will get back to you."

Sales Analysis: Competitor's Self-Inflicted Wounds

In this conversation, John clearly understood that the competitor was trying to pull the wool over his eyes, but the competitor was not prepared for intelligent questioning. He expected a simple-minded response: "Oh, you are going to reduce the price? Great! Where do I sign?" When he didn't get what he expected, he did not know where to go in the discussion or how to handle John's questions. The result was loss of credibility at the most critical point in time in the sales cycle.

Hopefully, you have a feeling now for how carefully executed trapping works. We have used two examples, but trapping can be applied to any anticipated competitive offensive in which you believe that the competition will be overconfident, negative about competitors, and maybe even arrogant. This is particularly important when your company is launching a new product. It's just not going to be perfect in terms of all the features or benefits that you would like to see it have, given your customer base and their needs. That means that you can expect your competitors to focus on the negatives, particularly if they are new to sales.

Note, however, that if you are up against a competitive Selling Fox, trapping will not work. Selling Foxes do not participate in negative selling and they do not operate precipitously. They are the trappers, not the prey. Their values keep them from engaging in unprofessional sales tactics and their intellects protect them from superficial endeavors. Additionally, trapping is a good source of entertainment and an important pastime for a Selling Fox, used routinely in almost every sales situation.

Trapping Is Fun

Professional selling, like any other job, has its ups and downs. There are the extremes—winning or losing an order—but in the middle is the wonderful experience of setting up competitors and watching them cause their own destruction. It is almost magical.

It is like going after a mouse. Night after night, you hear the little critter running around, and you see the signs of his presence the next day. Finally, you decide to set a trap. You go down to the hardware store, buy the little wooden death machine, and contemplate whether to use peanut butter or cheese to entice the little devil. After a few practice runs in which you nearly lose a finger, all is ready. Now you find just the right place to position it. With the trap securely in place, you retire for the evening. Suddenly it's 2 A.M. and you hear the snap. It cracks through the air, barely audible, yet you hear it as clearly as if it were right next to you. You spring to life, awake and alert. Never do you wake up so quickly, alive with anticipation. Without hesitation you scamper down the stairs, heading for the trap to witness your prize. Now, please don't take me literally, as I certainly don't like to see anything killed—even a mouse, neck broken in a pool of blood—but that's the spirit of competition.

A salesperson's own arrogance, unprofessional behavior, and negativity are the trap. That is what trapping is all about. Trust me on this:

you will know when a trap snaps, even if you are a thousand miles away. In fact, sometimes the customer will call you, perhaps saying something like this: "You will never believe what just happened. A competitor just came in for a meeting with us, throwing mud and challenging our ability to do a proper evaluation. Did he think that I was born yesterday? I have never seen such a lack of professionalism. We asked him to leave." Trapping is just wonderful!

Selling Fox Talk

As we discussed previously in this chapter, certain key or operative phrases are useful when setting traps:

Selling Fox Talk

Opening phrase: . . . *because we are new to working with each other, I would like to take a moment to share with you our company philosophy in building a new customer relationship.*

Talk about yourself. In that way, you are indirectly referencing the competition: *That kind of negative selling is off limits in our company . . . You will find us to be very straightforward. We will always level with you about what we can and cannot do.*

Loss of control by the customer: . . . *as if you as a manager could not do an evaluation of the various companies for yourself.*

Customer labeling—implication being that if a customer individual bites on the competitive offer, he or she is not experienced: *You're an experienced businessperson, John, and you know that if a product is properly priced, your supplier will have the margin needed to provide good service and support to you.*

Education: *If a company precipitously drops their price, it means that it has to be made up somewhere else, maybe cutting back on service. If that is not the case, the product may just have been overpriced to begin with.*

The Fox Ethos

Let's continue to build our list of Fox-like attributes:

The Fox Ethos

Foxes are extremely competitive by nature. Selling Foxes continually hone and employ techniques in the areas of negotiating, blocking, and trapping that will create competitive advantage for them.

Foxes are never superficial or unprofessional. Selling Foxes do not resort to negative selling or superficial ruses to win. They use their competitive selling abilities to outmaneuver and outsell the competition.

4

Selling at the Edge

Our major focus has been on the peaking or closing stages of a competitive sales cycle. It is an intense time when there is little margin for error; mistakes do occur, however, and sales situations will be compromised. When that happens, you fall from the lead to second place in a heartbeat. Unfortunately, there are no points awarded for second place. If you don't win, you lose, and losing is not acceptable to a Selling Fox.

Acknowledging the Possibility of Losing

In Chapter 1, we began by looking at the attitude of a Selling Fox, contrasting it to that of a more typical salesperson. If the attitude is wrong, no amount of technique or skill will compensate effectively. Here, the attitudinal component of selling centers on your views about losing. Most salespeople simply do not think about it. They avoid the negative, with the result that they are often caught off guard when the worst occurs. A Selling Fox knows that to acknowledge the negative is to be prepared, and that to be prepared is to maximize control over one's own destiny. The right to self-determination comes with a price; in this case the price is the ability and willingness to proactively acknowledge and prepare for a possible loss. A Selling Fox begins developing loss recovery plans early in the game. The following sections explain how.

Loss Recovery Plans and Techniques

The process begins with preparation, which is a "what if?" exercise.
What if:

- Without warning, the competition drastically reduces its price?
- The competition introduces new capabilities or a new product during the 11th hour of the sales situation?
- A new competitor comes on the scene with good contacts into the account? Who might they be, and what would they rely on to win?
- The competitor somehow changes the ground rules in the sales situation, altering the decision-making criteria—or alters the weighting (the emphasis placed on or importance of each criterion) dramatically in its favor? How might that occur, and what customer individuals might support such an effort?
- Customer funding somehow disappears?
- Your key supporter or ally leaves the company at just the wrong time?

These questions give you a feeling for the type of thinking that a Selling Fox typically goes through before a sales situation peaks. The Selling Fox not only anticipates most, if not all, of the possible negatives, but also formulates recovery approaches to these scenarios. He or she determines what resources might be required in a worst-case situation, and how to acquire those resources quickly when needed.

The process of loss recovery is not a difficult one, but there are certain aspects of it that need to be implemented with precision if you are to maximize the probability of success. As with all competitive situations in life, there are no guarantees, but the odds favor the best-prepared salesperson who possesses the skills to fully capitalize on that preparedness.

The first step in preparing for a potential loss relates to *time*.

It is absolutely critical that you detect a problem early and respond quickly.

I recently took up car racing, competing as a driver in the Ferrari 360 Challenge Series, running in the United States, Canada, and Italy. I learned the hard way that one of the first aspects of racing that a new

driver must master is control of the car at all times and under all imagi-
nable circumstances. For instance, coming out of a high-speed turn at
140 miles per hour and realizing that you have made a mistake is often
a white-knuckle experience. The back of the car slides out precipitously
and, as you work to regain control, you see a wall approaching. Your
heart rate increases to the max, like when you recognize that you are in
trouble in a highly competitive sales situation that is peaking, thrusting
you into a loss recovery mode.

Let's pause here and set the clock back for a moment relative to that
high-speed turn that I just mentioned. A mistake was made going into
that turn, or you wouldn't have found yourself losing control like that.
You could have been *off-line* (not being on the safest and fastest line
through the turn) or perhaps the mistake was an *early apex* (turning in
too early for the turn). If you recognize the mistake before reaching the
apex of the turn—no problem. You can carefully back off the throttle,
sacrificing a little exit speed coming out of the turn. Time, and possibly
position in the race, will be compromised, but that is a lot more acceptable than hitting a wall and being taken out of the race. And so it is with
selling—you must keep yourself in the game to the finish, having ex-
hausted all loss recovery options.

Timing Loss Recovery and Keeping Control

In sales, the apex of a competitive situation is marked by the customer's
buy commitment to a supplier. Sense that you are in trouble before that
point, and all is potentially recoverable. Realizing it after the apex is another story, as the risk of losing control of the car (or in this instance the
sales situation) rises dramatically.

In racing, we talk a lot about car control. In selling, the focus is not
on control, but rather managing the customer buying process to drive
competitive advantage and win business. In both cases, the issue when
things get hot is reaction time; it has to be almost reflex action. A Selling Fox is so rehearsed and attuned that loss recovery is second nature.

When you feel the back of the car sliding out on you, you must without hesitation countersteer and breathe off the throttle. There can be
no delay in that response—any hesitation and likely all will be lost.

In selling, this reaction translates to an immediate, no-hesitation implementation of your loss recovery plan. There is simply no substitute for being prepared. It is also worth noting that, because the present is a very volatile period of time in the competitive sales cycle, an order once lost and then saved can also be lost again. When a sales situation is peaking, the dynamics within the customer environment can be incredible. It is often a very emotional time, with personal, business, and political issues dominating people's thoughts and motivations.

In a race car, when you begin to lose control and quickly correct by countersteering, it is not uncommon for the car to jump into a slide going in the opposite direction. You swiftly gather up the car once again, trying to keep it on the track so that you can get back into the action without too much time lost. This can also be the case in loss recovery, in which you recover, take a deep breath, and feel that you're okay, only to find that the customer is suddenly not returning your calls. The car is sliding out of your control again. It's a horrible feeling, a "moment" as it is euphemistically referred to in racing, but all is not lost. You jump right back into a loss recovery mode, attempting to retrieve control by working the issues to a successful conclusion.

✖ *Never give up! Let the customer see your steadfast confidence in the quality of your solution.*

All too often, salespeople lose sales that could have been recovered. They lose because they accept defeat too early in the sales cycle. For many, the problem can be traced back to the attitudinal issue discussed earlier. If a salesperson does not acknowledge that he or she was outsold and really believes that the customer favors the competition because of price or because of lack of product functionality, it is pointless to launch a loss recovery plan.

✖ *Blaming external factors that are beyond your control is a way of giving yourself permission to lose.*

In a race, if you spin out but the car still can be driven, you get back onto the track and finish the race. It's a competitive attitude—you drive to win, and you can't win if you're not in the race anymore. Selling is no different!

Table 4.1 **Loss Recovery Timing**

Detection Time	Response Time	
	Fast	Slow
Early	Uneventful recovery	40% estimated recovery possibility
Late	Traumatic episode, 30% estimated recovery possibility	Loss of sale

How quickly you detect that you have a problem and how rapidly you respond both determine the type and severity of a potential loss situation. Table 4.1 shows how these two key timing factors work together.

As you can see, everything hinges on early detection and quick response. In competitive selling, early detection is achieved by faithfully adhering to the following principle:

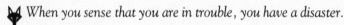

When you sense that you are in trouble, you have a disaster.

Follow your early instincts, which are often triggered by the following events:

- The customer is not returning your calls.
- The customer is not asking the types of detailed questions that should be asked if you were in good shape and the customer was planning to go with you.

Do not wait for confirmation of an unfavorable decision before taking action. Move, and move quickly—before you run off track and crash into a wall. If you are slow in your discernment of a problem, slow in your response, or both, the probability of a successful recovery will drop exponentially.

A Selling Fox knows that it is imperative to develop good instincts in this area, and that those instincts are acquired and honed only by thorough preparation and thoughtful execution. In time, you will know intuitively what to do and when to do it.

I learned this in a big way at VIR (Virginia International Raceway). I was a rookie. It was only my second race, so I was still on the steep part of the learning curve. With 17 turns to make and the need to know exactly where the braking points, turn-in points, throttle points, apexes, and track-out points for every turn were located, while driving at competitive speeds, I quickly realized that I had to create a mental image of the track. Preparation was not only necessary, but also a source of competitive advantage; this is why many drivers walk the track before a race and study each turn. They are doing their homework, just as every Selling Fox does in a competitive sales situation.

After years of experience, the ability to feel your way intuitively, including a certain sense for what will happen next in a competitive sales cycle, does develop. When this happens, you will sense, for example, when you should be talking to a particular customer individual. Often, if you don't call the customer, it is not uncommon for him or her to call you, verifying your instincts about the need to make the call.

Loss Recovery Principles

Behind every successful process is an operating philosophy, characterized by certain principles that contain the wisdom of the process. In loss recovery there are three key principles:

- *Get the timing right—detect early and respond quickly.*
- *Prepare and investigate—arm yourself with the facts.* Having anticipated what might go wrong, you expeditiously seek out your friendly contacts to understand what the actual situation is and why it developed. Recognize that this is best done off-site of the customer facility, and in person. It is imperative that you not compromise your contacts in any way. They have a fiduciary responsibility to their company. At the same time, you need to build an understanding of the situation. Who within the account is supporting the competition, and why?
- *Quickly and aggressively address the issues with new information.* Be certain to include some new piece of information that is *relevant to the customer*. It may focus on a new product announcement that is confidentially disclosed to the customer, or a planned partnership with

Table 4.2 **Loss Recovery Process**

Six Steps to Turning Business Around
1. Anticipate what could go wrong—there is no crystal ball, but most competitors are predictable.
2. Build a simple contingency plan based on the highest probability scenario, including the identification and allocation of resources to implement the plan.
3. Err on the side of early detection and rapid response—"turn on" the plan as soon as you have any indication of a problem.
4. Broaden your support base within the account—if the competition is changing the ground rules, you need to understand how they are doing it.
5. Inject new information into the buying process—at the very least, you may contain the competition.
6. Secure a commitment, recognizing that you may end up trial closing several times in order to get the information you need.

another company that will be advantageous to the customer, or it may be a resource commitment to the customer that was just approved by your senior management. The point is this: To turn an order around, without its being a negative reflection on the judgment of the customer decision-makers, you need to introduce the kind of new information that, had they had access to it earlier, would have caused them to consider going with you. It does not have to be earth-shaking in nature, just something relevant and new.

Loss Recovery Process

Loss recovery is not easy, but it is doable if you follow the principles that we have discussed, and adhere to the process outlined in Table 4.2.

Ranking Your Performance

Selling at the edge with strong tactical proficiency is characteristic of a Selling Fox, but where exactly is the edge and how do you get there safely?

Where the edge is for any one salesperson will vary with experience, ability, and personality. There is, however, one consistent method for assessing where the edge is for you. It is not complicated and requires no validation and reliability testing, just a bit of honest introspection and common sense. The process begins by looking at each competitive selling technique and honestly evaluating for yourself whether you find it manageable, difficult, or hard.

Manageable suggests that you are comfortable with a particular selling technique or tactic, like asking for an order, jumping objections, or perhaps trapping. You understand when to use the tactic or technique, how it is employed, and what to look for in terms of results. These techniques may have become intuitive for you.

Difficult indicates a degree of technical difficulty in understanding or deploying a particular technique. Often, role-playing to actually practice a technique, and additional management coaching are helpful in these instances.

Hard goes a step further. We are no longer simply talking about skills and knowledge, nor about the technical aspects of execution, but about the necessary attributes, or personality-related qualities, required to implement a particular sales approach. Think of these areas as serious attitudinal challenges. It may be that some techniques are basically intimidating for a person, or they may be inconsistent with his or her selling style or personal philosophy. Directly asking for an order, meeting with senior customer executives, or cold calling can fall into the hard category for a lot of people. The technique makes them very uncomfortable for reasons that are often personal or psychological in nature.

In any event, you are who you are and that is not bad. As a salesperson, the best thing you have going for you is *you*. The key is to recognize those aspects of competitive selling in which you shine as well as those which need some work.

Then you can develop your selling style and personal philosophy as you develop your sales skills. Style, personal philosophy, and sales skills need to work together—in concert—to create a balance between what you *can* do and what you are *willing* to do. To move forward in this process, think about where you are on the manageable-difficult-hard scale for each selling technique that we have discussed. Whenever you are going to do something competitive, pushing yourself to the edge of your personal limits, you need an objective means to determine where you are and where you want to go in terms of personal performance.

I have always loved cars and driving; however, I had never really thought about getting into automobile racing, and had never considered whether it might be suited to me or whether I'd be good at it. Then one day, I just took the leap. It was a difficult time for me. I was on the steep part of the learning curve in a series that had no novice class for rookies like me—that meant that from the moment the green flag dropped, I'd be running with the big dogs.

If you are too slow, you become dangerous, forcing faster drivers to attempt low-percentage (high-risk) passes during a race; otherwise they'd be slowed down to such a degree that other cars would catch up to them—not a good way to make new friends. Such a pass is inherently dangerous to both drivers, but in a highly competitive and aggressive series, it is to be expected. For me, minimizing the risk of these passes meant mastering (and I use the word loosely) each turn of a new track pretty quickly—getting to that intuitive point that helps a new driver to survive and learn. I needed to find out what I didn't know about each turn on the track in as few practice sessions as possible. By the time qualifying came around, the lines for each turn and my ability to be respectably competitive had to be established. That was a pretty daunting challenge.

My approach to racing was not very different from that of developing and implementing new competitive selling techniques. I rated each turn as manageable, difficult, or hard, but didn't get very far in the process before I experienced a serious setback. It happened at Road Atlanta, a difficult and sometimes scary track characterized by numerous elevation changes and one turn that was particularly challenging for me.

In turn 10b, you turn right and uphill, where the track then crests, leading to an approximate 200-foot bending drop down to the fastest turn on the track, which leads to the straight. Go over the crest at the wrong place and when you come down you can easily end up off the track. I did that twice during my practice runs, but because of my slower practice speeds I was able to recover.

During my fourth practice session, my driving had improved, and with it so had my speed and times. Going into turn 10a on one particular run, my times were the best that I had done so far on that track, which of course put me much faster into 10b, but the turn itself was not what was a problem for me. It was going over the crest that followed, and then down onto the straight, that required split-second precision. In a moment of preoccupation with the crest, while going into 10b, my focus shifted from the apex of 10b to a marker that we used on the bridge above the crest. I was thinking ahead, but doing so at the expense of focusing on the apex of 10b, which I missed by two feet. My concentration was dominated by the need to be in the right place going over the crest. Suddenly, the car wanted to track out drastically, but because I was offline I quickly ran out of asphalt. All this was happening after the apex—in the world of no recovery. Then the rear end of the race car broke loose, swinging around 180 degrees as I hit a tire wall on the driver's side. The force of the collision was so great that it caused my shoulder harnesses to stretch probably a foot. Fortunately, I only broke a rib due to the strong lateral impact, but my car was severely damaged.

For me, maneuvering the crest and dropping hill to the straight was definitely in the hard category—so much so that I became preoccupied with the task, compromising the earlier turn, 10b. Essentially, it was an attitude problem—the crest just weighed too heavily on me. In retrospect, I should have set a slower speed for that section of the track until I developed the right driving techniques. It would have eliminated a lot of stress and ultimately would have resulted in my becoming competitive and safe. Conceptually, for a brief moment in time, my driving ability exceeded my experience level, and the same can happen in selling.

Now, I always regard a performance problem as a skill/knowledge issue or an attitudinal consideration, and deal with it accordingly.

If you take a similar approach and rate your personal selling performance, you also will be able to:

- Determine what you need to do in order to move from difficult to manageable in a timely manner, as it relates to specific techniques.
- Identify, for you personally, what psychological barriers might exist that will inhibit your performance and success, which is your first step in addressing them.

It is very important that you take ownership of your own development, seeking out people who can coach and support you.

Your coach may be a sales manager or a high-performing, more experienced salesperson whom you trust. He or she will be someone who can review your actions and point out where you missed the apex. Sometimes it is someone who is not even in sales, but who nevertheless can serve as a good sounding board.

In my 30-plus years of selling experience, I have observed that the most difficult developmental challenges for salespeople are the internal, personality-related issues that require the help of another person. People are often not aware of these issues, which makes them particularly problematic.

Upon reviewing every detail of my mental attitude and driving performance, I had to admit to myself that when I hit the wall at Road Atlanta, it was due neither simply to my relative lack of skill, nor to my admittedly sparse knowledge of the track. An element that played heavily into the mix was *fear*. Fear of going off the track diverted my focus away from negotiating 10b safely, and that was my big error. Fear is what really put me out of the race, left me without a race car to drive, and could have cost me my life.

In selling, fear is also a factor for most of us. It may be fear of rejection by senior customer executives, fear of not knowing what to say in a difficult situation, fear of looking bad in front of your own management, or the ultimate fear of losing a sale. I believe that many salespeople don't make loss recovery contingency plans because of not wanting to articulate their fear of losing—not wanting to think about it.

That fear causes them to fail to acknowledge that they may lose. They therefore do not allow themselves to consider the downside or associate their thinking with a possible loss. They don't prepare, thereby increasing the probability that they will lose as they go into the most difficult turn of the sale.

In that sense, the old saying that outlook determines outcome and attitude determines action becomes very true.

For others, it is not fear that inhibits their performance, but rather the fact that they are too product-focused to see the larger view of customer and relationship management. They may lack the business or executive perspective necessary to sell solutions or to adopt a more consultative approach to selling, particularly when meeting with customer senior management.

Being too product-focused might at first sound like a training problem and maybe it is in some cases; but often it is an attitudinal problem

Table 4.3 **Self-Performance Rating**

Selling Techniques	M	D	H	Comments
Asking directly for an order				
Probing for objections				
Jumping objections				
Blocking the competition				
Trapping to negative selling				
Trapping to price discounting				
Trapping to product deficiencies				
Preparing for loss recovery				

Note: M = manageable, D = difficult, and H = hard

that is intrinsic to certain personality types. If an individual feels more comfortable dealing in the tangible product domain, it takes courage and determination to break out and expand into a broader world—one that encompasses business, strategic, financial, cultural, and political considerations that are often anything but tangible.

Manage Your Development–Rate Your Performance

As an introspective and developmental tool, rank your sales proficiency, using the manageable-difficult-hard scale, focusing on the techniques that we have covered so far. Table 4.3 is provided to help you rate your current performance.

✠ Sales Example 12–Self-Performance Rating Evaluation

Having completed a self-assessment, the next step is to look at those techniques that present problems for you, and create a self-development plan that defines your developmental goals, strategy, and tactics. For example, suppose that your assessment looks like the example provided in Table 4.4.

The profile reveals that four of the technique areas are manageable, three are difficult, and one is hard. Proportionally, this is not an un-

Table 4.4   **Example Self-Performance Rating**

Selling Techniques	M	D	H	Comments
Asking directly for an order			X	*Seems too forceful for me.*
Probing for objections	X			*No problem!*
Jumping objections	X			*No problem!*
Blocking the competition		X		*Difficult to read whether the ready, willing, and able states are or are not present.*
Trapping to negative selling		X		*This is a problem—trapping to behaviors.*
Trapping to price discounting		X		*Tough recognizing what type of customer individual will best respond to this form of trapping.*
Trapping to product deficiencies	X			*I'm comfortable trapping at the product level.*
Preparing for loss recovery	X			*I enjoy this and always do it.*

common profile. To increase sales performance, the salesperson who owns this profile needs to focus on the difficult and hard techniques, but with differing goals:

- *Hard technique goal* might be to move this technique into the manageable category within three months.
- *Difficult technique goal* might be to move these techniques into the manageable category within six months.

You may wonder why the time frame for moving the hard goal is shorter than that of conquering the difficult goal. The time frame for the hard goal is shorter because it is more critical in terms of securing business in the shortest sales cycles possible. People who do not explicitly close, for whatever reason, tend to protract sales cycles unnecessarily and diminish their control of the sales situation at the most critical point in time. In the best case, they give up the advantages that can be realized from early trial closes; in the worst case, they forfeit the opportunity to actually close the deal sooner or perhaps at all.

Achieving Self-Performance Goals

Developmental strategy: In the areas of closing and trapping to negative selling and price discounting, the salesperson should focus heavily on role-playing these situations with a sales manager or colleague, followed by assistance when on-site with the customer and when first attempting these new techniques.

In the area of blocking, the salesperson should use trial closing as the measurement device to know when any or all of the *ready, willing,* and *able* states are not present for the customer, followed by the employment of blocking—even if it is not required to block the competition. The purpose of this method is to observe the dynamics of the technique first-hand and build comfort with it.

Last, you need to build the appropriate tactics to operationalize the developmental strategy, including identifying any resources that will be necessary to support the effort. You may also want to create a time line that orders your tactics and works to the time frames set in the goal statements.

The right attitude: Be realistic about what you can and cannot do to maximize your tactical performance and selling success. As we cover additional competitive selling techniques, we will return to this type of developmental plan, so that by the end of this book, you will have not only new understanding of competitive selling, but the means and direction to capitalize on that knowledge to the fullest extent. This is how a Selling Fox operates—always learning, always performing to the max. For them, life is not about avoiding mistakes, but about learning the lessons from them. Have you ever seen a high-performing salesperson lose an order? Of course you have. A Selling Fox always reacts the same way:

- First, he or she completely internalizes the loss, accepting full personal responsibility for it. A Selling Fox does not blame the product, the customer, the company, or anything or anyone else. In this way, a Selling Fox takes complete ownership of failures, for in the long term, they will become assets in the form of wisdom acquired through those losses and the lessons that will be learned from them.
- Second, having understood exactly what occurred to cause the loss, a Selling Fox closes the door on the experience so that it does not impact future performance. In racing to win, you cannot drive in your rearview mirror; nor can you in selling.

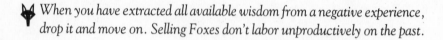 *When you have extracted all available wisdom from a negative experience, drop it and move on. Selling Foxes don't labor unproductively on the past.*

Their image of themselves is in no way tarnished by failure, as they know who they are and what they believe in.

- Selling Foxes manage their egos; they don't let their egos manage them. They do not suffer from an enlarged ego that all too often masks insecurity. Therefore, loss of a sale for them does not cause an additional loss—that of self-esteem.

We all know some people who are primarily concerned about their image and always blame other people, events, or things for their failures, but take total personal credit whenever anything goes right.

Selling Foxes have neither the time nor the patience for such a shallow existence; nor do most senior customer executives when dealing with salespeople. Too many people in sales brag about their executive-level contacts—but in reality, they have cultivated few (if any) trust-based relationships. They will never be Selling Foxes because they live a superficial professional life.

Contrasting Fox-like traits with those of non-Foxes is important, not only in the area of driving personal and rapid self-development, but also in establishing and maintaining customer executive relationships. Fox-like characteristics, or the Fox ethos, if you will, are especially important in professional selling, quickly separating the true professional from the amateur.

The Fox Ethos

We continue our list of Fox-like attributes:

The Fox Ethos

Selling Foxes know that to acknowledge the negative is to be prepared, and that to be prepared is to maximize control over their own destiny.

Selling Foxes are so rehearsed and attuned that loss recovery is second nature.

Foxes never give up! Let the customer see their steadfast confidence in the quality of their solution.

Foxes practice continual self-development. It is very important that they take ownership of their own development, seeking out people who can coach and support them.

Selling Foxes don't labor unproductively on the past.

Selling Foxes manage their egos; they do not let their egos manage them.

5

Calling High

Getting to the top of a customer organization and staying there requires the right set of individual capabilities coupled with the right process. It is an advanced aspect of selling that is a challenge for everyone, but there is a Fox-like way of succeeding.

Executive Relationship Principles

Selling Foxes follow three key principles—fundamental truths that serve as a guide to establishing and maintaining executive-level relationships:

1. *When it comes to executive calling, you will be as successful as you are executive-like yourself.* This does not mean that you need to be an executive or have twenty-plus years of business experience, but it does suggest that possessing certain executive qualities is essential to relationship management. To be specific, we are talking about certain Fox-like characteristics.
2. *When it comes to executive calling, you will be as successful as the value that you can provide to an executive.* Providing value to a customer senior executive and his company occurs in two forms:

   - First is the personal value that you provide as an individual.
   - Second is the business value that you provide through your company.

Positioning yourself as a relevant resource, both at the personal and professional levels, is critical to true relationship management.

3. *When it comes to executive calling, you will be as successful as your calling process is effective.* Making that first contact correctly can be critical to winning a competitive deal or penetrating and developing a potentially significant account. A misstep at that point will be very difficult to recover from and could possibly even cripple your sales efforts. To ensure that this does not happen, it's best to rely on a proven process, built on a foundation of Fox-like behavior and value, that will guide you step by step each time you call high in a new account.

What you will find is that all success in relationship management comes down to the following three factors:

1. Who you are as a person
2. The value you provide
3. The process you implement

In its very simplest form, if you work to the following three operative words, before, during, and after an executive call, you will always stay on track with what is most important in relationship management.

Principles – Value – Process

When it comes to executive calling, you will be as successful as you are executive-like yourself.

It is not uncommon for salespeople to do a great job of setting up a meeting with a customer senior manager, only to find it to be a one-time event. Even if value is provided during that meeting, it will not lead to subsequent meetings if a positive person-to-person relationship is not quickly formed. It may appear difficult given the short amount of time that you and an executive are together, but it is definitely manageable if you know what to focus on during the exchange.

A Fox, by virtue of being a Fox, will always recognize another Fox under the right circumstances.

It doesn't take long and it is always a binary judgment that accompanies the observation. Foxes focus less on what you are saying and more on who you are as an individual. In that respect, they can extrapolate why you're saying what you are saying—they look for the motivation behind the words. This certainly is not to say that all senior managers are Foxes; in fact, very few are. Those who are, however, represent the driving force within their companies, and they are therefore the most important people with whom you can align to advance your sales efforts.

This means that in looking for the right people on whom you'd call in a company, you should first seek to identify the executive Fox who wields influence where you need it. A salesperson who is not yet a Selling Fox needs to become adept in identifying and tracking executive Foxes. They are often difficult to spot, but if you become a Selling Fox, as evidenced by your behavior, it will be a lot easier because customer Foxes will most often reveal themselves to you. They will not do this by saying, "I'm a Fox," of course, but you'll spot them by their openness to you and their Fox-like behavior that will be observable.

Fox Characteristics

Listed here are the core characteristics that signal to a customer executive Fox that you are also a Fox. They are more important than most people could imagine, for they shape the attitudes and personal philosophy of an individual. That personal philosophy, when combined with a Selling Fox's personal business development system, which we revisit in Chapter 10, comprises the full force of their competitiveness.

Not Egocentric

 Foxes enjoy a distinct lack of ego, running silent most of the time. They do not seek or need recognition—they are interested in results.

They are definitely high-level players in the company, yet they may or may not have the title that awards the level of influence they wield behind the scenes by pulling strings that are often not visible to others. Therefore, any form of recognition or visibility might have a compromising effect on them. You cannot possess and exude Fox-like values and service a big ego at the same time.

We all recognize that ego is a natural component of our personalities as salespeople, but if we allow it to become too great a drive in how we sell, it will also become a self-limiting liability.

Always remember that people who view themselves as the center of the universe are not Foxes. Such people may be powerful but are rarely good leaders with an ability to inspire, coalesce, and coach others.

Good Listener

 Foxes enjoy strong listening ability, which is generally a part of their natures given their natural focus on others rather than themselves.

Conceptually, Foxes place themselves below the person speaking, discerning intent by looking beyond the spoken words. During an initial business meeting, with only a short time together, neither person can make an accurate determination as to whether it is appropriate to trust the other. Trust must be earned, but in the absence of time and the opportunity to build trust, how do you proceed? The next best thing is to accurately assess a person's motivations and the values by which he or she operates, and to be clear about your own motivations and values. This enables you to approximate how a customer executive may respond to future challenges or issues; more importantly, however, it gives you the opportunity to communicate that you sincerely care about the customer and his or her company needs. Keep the following facts in mind:

* You cannot care and not listen.
* Most people want to know that you care *before* they care about what you know.

High Integrity

 Foxes enjoy a high level of personal integrity—a much overlooked and misunderstood source of competitive advantage. Foxes tend to seek out and align with other people of high integrity.

Let's look at an example. If a salesperson is willing to bend the truth to make a sale, what does it tell you from the point of view of a customer executive Fox?

Point 1: Take away the euphemistic lenses and recognize that bending the truth, managing information, applying inappropriate spin, so to speak, or leaving out information is, in its simplest sense, lying. People who lie are not to be trusted, ever!

Point 2: Suppose you assume that Point 1 above does not apply. Maybe you rationalize, "We all bend the truth a little, so what is the harm?" True, you have jumped over the integrity issue, but what about the salesperson's *motivation*, always a key factor to a Fox? Is it to help the customer, as the priority? No, it is to get an order. To a person of low integrity, helping the customer is secondary or incidental—just the necessary vehicle to accomplishing the goal of securing an order. That is not to say that a Fox will not do business with such a person, but it does mean that he or she will not become unnecessarily dependent on that salesperson; the consequence is that the salesperson will be thus excluded from the inner circle, or Power Base, of the executive Fox. Nor will Foxes likely reveal themselves as Foxes or share what motivates them in terms of personal agenda, which is explained in more detail in the following paragraphs. All this means that when a Fox senses that a salesperson is manipulative, significant guards go up that inhibit the building of a trust-based relationship.

All of this is good news for a Selling Fox, whose Fox-like ethos creates a nontraditional source of competitive advantage.

Mission Driven

 Foxes enjoy a connection to mission. They attach a higher-order purpose to anything significant that they pursue.

Ever wonder why you were born, what purpose exists for your being on the planet? Such questions haunt mission-driven people at some point in their lives, as they strive to get beyond the superficial aspects of life and tap into its essence.

Watch a Fox in action and you will always see him or her distilling a difficult situation down to its essential elements. This produces an encapsulated comprehension that creates immediate manageability. It boils down to understanding what is really important.

The Personal Agenda

A Fox knows that just as that encapsulation of essential elements applies to complex situations or problems, it also applies to people. What is *really* important to you, as it relates to your job? Many people ask this type of question, but Foxes usually have good answers, which creates a context for everything important that they do in their profession and in life. This is called their *personal agenda*. If you are a salesperson of high integrity and can provide value that advances a customer Fox's personal agenda, you will gain a very influential ally.

Ask, "What is the mission of an egocentric person?" The true answer will center on some form of self-gratification. Ask the same question to an individual lacking integrity and, by definition, you will receive some form of superficial answer, if not an outright lie. In both cases, the ability to discern the meaning or purpose of anything is simply not there. If it is, at its best, it is greatly diminished. Personal implications notwithstanding, this means that such an individual cannot really understand or relate to a true Fox, nor to his or her personal agenda; this trait cripples the relationship before it is ever formed.

These four core characteristics that identify you as a Selling Fox will always be present together:

- Not egocentric
- Good listener
- High integrity
- Mission driven

Although the world may discount one or more of the key characteristics, Foxes do not. They will recognize such characteristics and you as Fox-like, and most often invite you to go to the next step in building the relationship.

As such, your success at the executive levels will be significantly influenced by who you are or who you as an individual aspire to be.

Still, it is your job to find the appropriate Foxes within an account and make contact with them as early in the sales cycle as possible. To assist you, I recommend that you employ the Fox Evaluator™[1], a highly usable sales tool for determining whether a customer individual is a Fox or whether he or she is inside or outside the Power Base.

Finding the Power Base

The Power Base consists of individuals tightly networked with a Fox. They may reside within or among departments or divisions of a customer's company. They often share a common philosophy and usually have very compatible, closely aligned personal agendas. In this way, people within the Power Base can tap the Fox's power by association, increasing their own influence.

In identifying the Power Base, we are looking at the distribution of influence, *not* authority. Foxes wield tremendous influence, but again, may not reside at the top of the organization, nor possess titular authority in the executive ranks. Rarely does their level of influence correspond with the level of their authority, the former being disproportionately greater than the latter. They can work in exception to company policy and are rarely surprised by significant events within the organization.

 Bond with the right Fox, and you will likely have access to the entire executive team of a company.

Go Fox Hunting

Following is the Fox Evaluator in Table 5.1, an efficient tool for finding and identifying a Fox.

When it comes to executive calling, you will be as successful as the value that you provide.

We've talked a lot about providing *value* to a customer. Value is a critical ingredient to operating successfully in the executive world, but what is it, exactly? Assessing the existence of value provided requires two bilateral or reciprocal components:

---

[1]Fox Evaluator is a trademark of Holden International.

Table 5.1 **The Fox Evaluator**

Rate each item using the –2 to +2 values. Then total your answers and use the probable results at the bottom of the page to determine whether your contact is a FOX, in the Power Base, or outside the Power Base.

Score	Definition
+2	I am confident this is true.
+1	This is most likely true.
0	I don't know.
–1	I doubt this is true.
–2	I am confident that this is not true.

Contact's Name:

Fox Evaluator Questions	Score
1. _____ has exerted influence outside of his/her organizational authority.	
2. _____ has knowledge of his/her company's mission and business goals, as evidenced in his/her working to directly or indirectly advance them.	
3. _____ is an effective risk taker, in terms of his/her ability to assess and manage risk.	
4. _____ demonstrates integrity in terms of being unwilling to compromise his/her company or individuals within the Power Base® to advance his/her own aspirations.	
5. _____ is a good listener.	
6. _____ can appropriately and successfully work in exception to company policy.	
7. _____ influences important decisions before they are formally made.	
8. _____ has a close relationship with others who possess expertise that he/she personally does not have, but that can be important.	
9. _____ is not arrogant about his/her knowledge or accomplishments as evidenced by his/her willingness to have others receive the credit for accomplishments.	
10. _____ is diplomatic in how he/she operates, as evidenced by rarely taking people on in a confrontational manner.	

Total Your Score

Score	Results
+14 to +20	Congratulations! You have found a FOX
+7 to +13	He/she is not a FOX, but is in the Power Base
–20 to +6	He/she is outside the Power Base

- The personal value that you provide to a customer executive and the personal value that he or she provides back to you
- The business value that your company provides to a customer and the business value that the customer provides back to your company

This bilateral nature of the value at the individual and company levels is important to recognize and understand, as it becomes the real measure of whether you are being successful in your executive calling efforts. Salespeople who are not Selling Foxes tend to think that executive calling is all about getting a meeting, or at best being able to secure a follow-up meeting with high-level people. Although that is certainly important, what they tend to miss is

- Who are the *right* executives to contact—who are the Foxes, the approvers, and the decision-makers?
- What value can you provide them, and how do you bring that to their attention?
- What value do you need to receive in return from them and how do you get it?

Very few salespeople actually have a sense for what they want from a customer executive, other than some indication of that person's general support for their sales efforts. What you need to determine early on is the *nature* and *extent* of the executive support that you'll need to ensure your success. Building a precise understanding in this area is the key to unlocking how to actually secure that support in the shortest amount of time.

Creating Balanced Value

Establishing personal value falls under the umbrella of an initial value statement that positions your company as a potential resource to the customer. Recently I sent an e-mail to an executive of a multibillion dollar company with which my company had not yet worked. We saw the potential but needed to position ourselves properly first in order to initiate an executive dialog.

When we were ready to move forward, our approach was simple. It followed along the lines of, "If your corporate intent is to become the dominant provider in (I referenced a specific industry), displacing (a specific industry leader), we believe that we can provide significant assistance, while deepening our market penetration in the process."

When this senior executive received the e-mail, he already knew the name of my company based on our market presence. He also knew that his company's primary competitor in their industry, whom I had referenced, had recently acquired one of our competitors—thus the stage was set for us to make contact.

Construct a Focused and Balanced Value Statement

If you examine it closely, you will see that my brief value statement was surgically focused, creating a positioning for all that would follow. We talk more about the mechanics of executive calling when we address process (later in this chapter), but suffice it to say that the e-mail was well received, and we subsequently opened discussions as to how we would work together.

As simple a value statement as it was, you will note that it was *balanced*. I was clear about what we wanted in return—increased market penetration. By stating your motivation, you save the executive from having to figure it out, which saves time and helps to avoid confusion. It also begins to establish your operating style. From the first contact through to negotiating the terms of an order, you should be doing everything possible to comply with the principle of balanced value.

> *Every value contribution made or proposed should have a reciprocating component to help establish and maintain approximate equilibrium in the relationship.*

If you follow this principle, the alignment of your interests to those of the customer will occur much more quickly and smoothly, not to mention the advantages that it will provide later in negotiating terms and conditions along with pricing. Help with fashioning a value statement is provided in a template in this chapter in the section titled "Balancing Business Value."

With the initial umbrella value statement in place, you are ready to focus on *personal value*, which is where the journey to building and maintaining executive relationships really begins. Again, it is bilateral in nature, consisting of the following components:

Value you provide to an executive
- The business insight that you can provide to the executive
- The potential for you to advance an executive's personal agenda

Value an executive provides to you
- The sales support provided to you when the executive is characterized as a supporter or ally
- The potential for an executive to advance your personal agenda

Let's look at each of these components and how they interrelate:

Value You Provide to an Executive

The Business Insight That You Can Provide to the Executive

As a salesperson, you have the opportunity to work with many companies and perhaps multiple industries, which enables you to develop significant insight into what is driving various markets, new and emerging trends, and the changing positioning of competitors. Such positioning often consists of the value competitors provide to the marketplace, their pricing, and the uniqueness of the value they offer. It is this type of insight that will allow you to speak with a customer executive and talk about emerging market trends and their potential impact on the business practices of the executive's company.

The Potential for You to Advance an Executive's Personal Agenda

A personal agenda is that aspect of an individual's professional role that he or she has internalized or taken to heart. It is a professional expression of personal mission, as it relates to the workplace. In the case of a Fox, an agenda always plays in concert with what is good for his or her company. Examples of personal agendas are:

- The success of an executive's company or department
- Promotion, in terms of vertical mobility

- Preservation or the achievement of lifestyle goals such as income or leisure time
- Prevailing in a power struggle (political competition between two individuals)
- Ensuring the success of a particular project or initiative

Whatever the personal agenda of an executive is, it is your responsibility to understand it, and if appropriate, advance it. I say *appropriate* because there are executives who are quite willing to advance themselves at the expense of their company's best interest or the people around them, including salespeople. Such people can be very powerful, but are not Foxes. It can be tempting to get behind them, but you must keep in mind that an executive willing to compromise his or her own company will not hesitate to compromise you and your company. Selling Foxes do not align with such people.

Value an Executive Provides to You

The Sales Support Provided to You When the Executive Is Characterized As a Supporter or Ally

A supporter is a customer individual who recognizes the value that you can provide at the personal and/or company levels, and as a result is willing to provide sales support relative to a specific vendor evaluation or sales situation.

An ally recognizes that same value, along with the presence of shared values, which creates a more trust-oriented, long-term relationship. The result is an executive who will support you in any and all sales efforts, thus becoming your best referral—a trusted ally. Making these and other relationship assessments quickly and objectively requires a particular sales tool—the Contact Evaluator™² shown in Table 5.2.

Characterizing Relationship Support

As you can see, the Contact Evaluator is a relationship support indicator. It enables you to assess rapidly whether a customer individual is:

---

²Contact Evaluator™ is a trademark of Holden International.

Table 5.2 **The Contact Evaluator**

Rate each item using the values −2 to +2. Then total your answers and use the probable results at the bottom of the page to rate the strength of your relationship with each contact.													
Account Name:						**Your Contacts** (fill in contact names, one column per contact)							
−2 Almost never	**−1** Rarely	**0** Sometimes	**+1** Often	**+2** Almost always									
1. My discussions with _____ touch upon potential opportunities beyond the current business opportunity.													
2. _____ utilizes me or my company as a nontraditional resource through which value can be derived.													
3. _____ makes an extra effort to assist me in cost-justifying the value that we can contribute.													
4. _____ introduces or references me to influential people in the account.													
5. _____ has a clear strategy for establishing us as the preferred supplier.													
6. _____ utilizes internal contacts to provide me with business insights and information of a privileged nature.													
7. _____ openly discusses his/her company's plans, projects, and personnel with me.													

continued

Table 5.2 **Continued**

	-2 Almost never	-1 Rarely	0 Sometimes	+1 Often	+2 Almost always	Your Contacts (fill in contact names, one column per contact)							
8. _____ can articulate my personal or company's long-term strategy for building a relationship with his/her company and how the current opportunity contributes to its advancement.													
9. _____ takes the initiative in assisting me in the current business development opportunity.													
10. I feel my relationship with _____ transcends the business development opportunity at hand.													
14 to 20 = Ally (A) 4 to 13 = Supporter (S) −10 to 3 = Nonsupporter (N) −20 to −11 = Opponent (O) **Totals**													

- An ally—provides significant support to any sales situation
- A supporter—provides support specifically to sales situations
- A nonsupporter—is a neutral influence
- An opponent—is a customer individual who opposes your sales efforts

The potential for an executive to advance your personal agenda is another value that an executive can provide. Winning deals and turning lost business around does great things for a salesperson's career and pocketbook, of course, but still it is easy for salespeople to operate in a career-limiting manner. In some companies, they are misunderstood, viewed as overpaid employees who work short hours and do little more than buy lunch as a liaison to the customer base. It is no surprise that Selling Foxes would never be found working for such companies, but even in the more customer-centered organizations, it is easy to suboptimize your career or compromise advancement of your personal agenda.

What Is Your Personal Agenda?

Foxes possess absolute clarity in this area, as you will recall from our discussion of mission. Agenda advancement is an important part of overall compensation, in some cases eclipsing that of money after the dollars have reached a certain required level. I once knew a salesperson who was very active in his community and chose to turn down promotions in order not to relocate. He had integrated a local business community orientation and social life into his selling that was very successful, resulting in an optimum personal lifestyle for himself and his family. Figure 5.1 provides a visual conceptualization of balanced value.

 Creating balance in the exchange of value produces equilibrium in the relationship that leads to stability and longevity.

Managing this balance requires sales tools that enable you to quickly and objectively assess balance. The Currency Tabulator™[3] and Contact Evaluators perform that function, as shown in Figure 5.2.

The Value of Personal Currency

The Currency Tabulator is a value indicator. It is based upon a concept that views a salesperson as an asset that will either appreciate or depreciate throughout a sales cycle. The more currency you have, the more value you can potentially provide to the customer. If you provide value in the right manner, your currency grows.

The Currency Tabulator, shown in Table 5.3, is another highly usable sales tool that consists of 10 questions, with the results expressed in terms of three levels of currency:

[3]Currency Tabulator™ is a trademark of Holden International.

Figure 5.1 **Creating Balanced Value**

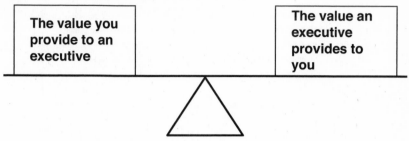

Figure 5.2 **Balance Assessment Sales Tools**

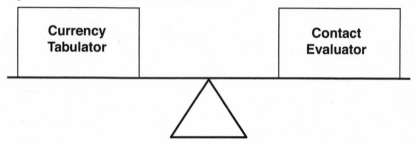

- Executive level
- Middle management level
- Operations level

Simply stated, in order to be executive credible, you need to be at an executive currency level. The same holds true with the middle management and operations levels, in terms of being effective at those levels within the customer's organization.

The goal within any account is to build executive-level allies and supporters. Specifically, you need to build ally and supporter relationships with customer executive Foxes and people within the Power Base.

Your ability to accomplish this will be a function of your own currency level, thereby creating bilateral value that is balanced. If you have anything less than executive-level currency, you will most likely not be able to develop executive-level allies or supporters. There are certainly no hard and fast rules, but in general, personalities notwithstanding, the impact of currency levels on relationship quality, as it relates to value, looks like the following:

Table 5.3 **The Currency Tabulator**

Respond to all the items in reference to a single client. You must be able to give an unqualified 100% positive response to an item to award the points indicated. If you cannot give an unqualified 100% positive response to an item, score the item 0. In-between scores are *not valid*. Total your score below.

Account Name:

Currency Tabulator Questions	Score
1. If you have an ally[1] within the customer's executive management team, enter a score of 10 points; if he or she is a Fox[2], score 15 points.	
2. If you have a supporter[3] within the customer's executive management team, enter a score of 5 points, if he or she is a Fox[4], score 10 points.	
3. If you can correctly identify the top 3 trends within your customer's industry, enter a score of 10 points.	
4. If you can correctly identify your customer's top 3 competitors, enter a score of 10 points.	
5. If you can articulate the customer's corporate goals and objectives, enter a score of 10 points.	
6. If you can describe your customer's value chain, as they view their marketplace, enter a score of 10 points.	
7. If you can identify the personal agenda (a political or organizational aspiration) of the corporate Fox within your customer's organization, enter a score of 10 points.	
8. If you have uncovered a power struggle or power play within your customer's organization, enter a score of 10 points.	
9. If you have made 100% of your quota for 5 or more consecutive years within your company, enter a score of 10 points.	
10. If you have quick access to your own executive management, enter a score of 10 points.	

Total your score

If your score fell into the following ranges	Your currency strength can be considered
85 to 105	Executive level
65 to 84	Middle management level
64 or below	Operations level

[1]Please use the Contact Evaluator to make this determination.
[2]Please use the Fox Evaluator to make this determination.
[3]Please use the Contact Evaluator to make this determination.
[4]Please use the Fox Evaluator to make this determination.

- Executive-level currency generally advances supporter relationships at the customer executive levels and ally and supporter relationships at the middle management and operations levels.
- Executive-level currency with a proven track record within an account, which dramatically increases currency, often leads to the formation of executive allies.
- Middle management currency generally advances supporter relationships at the customer middle management levels and ally and supporter relationships at the operations levels.
- Operations-level currency generally advances ally and supporter relationships at the operations levels.

You can see that highly competitive sales situations or sales opportunities within major accounts require that you build executive-level currency in a timely manner. For more transaction-driven, shorter-cycle sales situations, middle management currency may be fine, again assuming that you are not up against stiff competition.

Balancing Business Value

This same concept of balance applies to the business value that your company provides to a customer and the value that they provide back to your company. In both cases, it can be viewed in qualitative and quantitative terms. A value statement is qualitative in nature, while a value proposition is quantitative. The following template tools will help you construct these expressions of value and apply them to accounts:

> ### Value Statement Template
> Based on our experience in (*doing what, generally*), we have the ability to (*contribute what, specifically*) resulting in (*type of business improvement*) for (*customer*).

> ### Value Proposition Template
> Beginning (*implementation date*) as a result of our (*product/service/capability*), (*customer*) will be able to (*do what*) resulting in (*quantified business improvement*) for (*total investment cost*), with the economic payback achieved within or by (*time*). We will document our delivered value by measuring (*results tracking parameters*).

Succinct expressions of value, such as those outlined in the preceding templates, can be very compelling, but how do you acquire the business insight to draft such statements and propositions? The goal is to have the customer internalize your offering or solution—to see and feel its real value. For that to happen, you need to do the necessary research to create a context that has already been internalized by the customer, often found in the following areas of the customer's business:

- *Business direction:* Understanding the company's plans for internal expansion, divestiture, acquisition, shifts in market focus, and so on, provides a backdrop in terms of context.
- *Major initiatives and problems:* Important projects that will advance a company's business direction, or solutions to difficult business problems, can provide both insight and an opportunity for you to create value beyond what you're offering or beyond that which your solution itself provides. It may be that a much larger company investment can be protected or enhanced as a result of your solution, which means your solution then takes on a larger strategic and financial significance to that customer.
- *Financial opportunities and problems:* Each of the aforementioned major initiatives or problems will be tied directly or indirectly to positive or negative financial impact. Understanding the nature of this impact allows you to draw a line from your solution to the customer's bottom line.

Sometimes you will see opportunities that the customer does not see, but for the most part, value positioning is a bridging exercise. You start by building a customer profile. The profile should briefly identify information such as the customer's strategic direction, position in the marketplace, major competitors, and areas of competitive differentiation. Hopefully, in doing that you will uncover major initiatives, as well as problems that perhaps need to be addressed. Basically, you're working to understand their company business plan through various discussions with customer individuals.

This approach usually applies to larger accounts, but in short-cycle sales situations there is still room for some value positioning, which more often tends to be a bit generic in nature. Generally speaking, a company's marketing department develops such positioning. With a quick-start profile in place, you are ready to build a value continuum that starts with your solution, then moves to its impact on some corporate initiative and then to some financial expression of that impact. The customer impact continuum in Figure 5.3 shows the relationship between these components.

The key is to show how your solution will trigger a disproportionately larger positive impact on the customer's business.

In one case I recall, the customer was very concerned about earnings per share. The chief financial officer (CFO) was a corporate Fox who was keenly interested in improving the earnings picture along with any initiatives that could drive such an improvement. After several discussions with middle management, it became clear that a particular product line was producing disproportionately high profits in comparison with their traditional business, and that it was underleveraged from a business point of view—no one was focusing on how to grow that smaller part of their business.

The bridging opportunity was to connect the supplier's solution to increasing revenues for that product line, thereby enabling the salesperson to build a very strong value proposition. The focus of the value proposition was on earnings per share. It detailed how one dollar of revenue in the underleveraged product line was equivalent to three dollars of revenue from the company's traditional business, based upon the per-dollar margins of the underleveraged product line as compared to traditional business lines.

Stated simply, the underleveraged product line produced three times the profit of their traditional business line. As a result, increasing its sales produced an accelerated positive effect on earnings.

Producing the value proposition for this opportunity required that certain assumptions be made and that a goal be established, in terms of impact; this is something that you will face quite often as you create value propositions. Even with good assumptions that the customer agrees with, you will not always be able to quantify value. Yet, quantification is required in order to project real and tangible value. The answer is to establish a reasonable goal. In the case of our example, that was an estimate of a potential increase in earnings per share.

Figure 5.3   **Customer Impact Continuum**

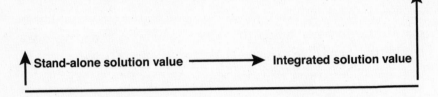

It is important to point out to the customer that this is not a commitment, but a project goal. Your commitment is to do everything possible to help them to realize that goal. Remember that you are trying to draw a line from your offering to business impact by enhancing something that the customer is counting on, or could count on, to strengthen and grow that customer's business.

When it comes to executive calling, you will be as successful as your calling process is effective.

This executive calling process is designed to guide you through the necessary steps to establishing and maintaining executive relationships, subject to the principles by which you sell and the value that you are able to deliver.

Principles – Value – Process

You will recall that as in any process, if you skip steps, you will probably have to make them up later, thus decreasing your effectiveness and slowing down the process. At the same time, don't hesitate to modify and shape the process to suit your personal selling style, the types of accounts that you pursue, and the nature of your business.

The Seven-Step Executive Calling Process

The following is a seven-step executive calling process that is designed to assist you in building a multi-executive, multilevel support base within an account:

> **Seven-Step Executive Calling Process**
> 1. Preparing for contact
> 2. Executive preconditioning
> 3. Making contact
> 4. The initial executive meeting
> 5. Defining your support base objectives
> 6. Developing your value proposition
> 7. The value acknowledgment executive meeting

1. Preparing for Contact

A Selling Fox always works to win a battle before it is fought, and executive calling is no exception. Here, pre-preparation is critical. If the stage is not set properly, you will not succeed in a timely manner. The following is what is needed for pre-preparation:

- You need an understanding of the customer's business sufficient to support the generation of a preliminary bilateral value statement. To gain such an understanding, read the appropriate trade publications and business newspapers; also research the company's web site. Most important, talk to people—anyone who can provide you with information to help give you the insight you need, like partner companies, their employees, board of directors, anyone at all, including their competition.
- You also need a feeling for who might be the appropriate customer Fox within the account for you to target. It's okay to get this wrong, as you will still most probably land somewhere within the Power Base, or the Fox's inner circle, if you will.

  Caution: What you do not want to do is pursue a meeting with the highest-level person you can identify. The higher you go, the more difficult it will be to construct a value message as it relates to your business. There will be simply too many other factors that could contribute to or detract from the business impact that serves as the basis for your value statement. It is always a balance between getting high enough to focus on global or corporate initiatives, and also being low enough to have more of a direct, versus indirect, impact on those initiatives.

To accomplish this objective, speak to all those indicated previously, but also talk with other suppliers (not your competitors!) as to who has driven significant buy decisions in the past in that company—basically, go Fox hunting, using the tools we have provided to you.

- Finally, you'll need an ability to recognize and relate to the customer executive you plan to contact. Learn as much as possible about the individual—his or her personality, hobbies, management style, and any past history or contact with your company.

2. Executive Preconditioning

In many cases, for an executive to take the time to consider meeting with you, a certain amount of perceived value or the potential for value must exist. This judgment will be based upon what he or she knows about your company. If your marketing department is on its game, this will not be a problem. If not, you will have to compensate. Several methods for accomplishing this are

- Construct an opening statement and explanation with an e-mail that positions what your company has done in the industry in order to help establish credibility and potential value to the customer.
- Find another executive who knows the person you want to contact, and who is willing to provide some endorsement for your company along similar lines.
- Have one of your own company executives make contact first with the target executive, again with the same intent. Recognize that this will generally require that same company executive to be involved in the initial meeting with the customer executive, so be sure he or she is willing to participate.

3. Making Contact

The first point in initiating contact with a customer executive is to view the executive's personal assistant as you would the executive. Use the same value messaging as you would with the executive. To do anything less is a strategic error.

The nature of that initial contact could be by e-mail, which often has the added benefit of going directly to the executive. Alternately, you might use a telephone call or introductory letter. My preferences for contact fall in the order listed here.

Your goal at this point is to get the meeting, but don't be discouraged if you are referred down the chain. If you've managed to identify a possible Fox and are in the Power Base, no problem.

4. The Initial Executive Meeting

Your dress for the meeting should be very professional—business attire. Even if the customer's organization has a casual dress policy, go for the professional image.

As you open the meeting, work through the pleasantries with sincerity. This is one area in which your pre-preparation will really pay off.

Remember that your goal at this stage in the process is to capture interest, build insight, and link to a follow-up executive meeting.

Next:

- Transition into the business focus with a brief introduction to your company and its contribution to the customer's industry, and present your prepared value statement.
- Then move the customer executive to center stage, to assist you in developing a better understanding of his or her business, direction, and challenges, as they relate to what you do. Make it crisp and sincere.
- Ask sensible questions that convey understanding on your part, helping to establish your credibility, and also to equip yourself with what you need to enhance your value statement and launch a competitive sales campaign.
- Listen *very carefully* to the executive's responses to your questions and to anything else he or she might offer in the way of general comments about the company's business or goals.
- Try to discern, through good listening and careful questioning, who else you need to be speaking with in the account, and what their relationship is to the customer executive.
- Be certain that your personal values and your integrity, which we discussed earlier, come across to the executive. He or she must develop some insight into who you are as an individual, as well as what you represent as a company, in order to begin to determine whether you can be trusted. This is particularly true of a Fox.

- Steer away from product discussions or technical issues. Keep the direction focused on the business points on which the executive has focused during the discussion. Work in tandem with him or her to define the value proposition goal, if at all possible. Tangibility will come from that and should not come from the product unless the customer executive directs you there.
- Create a logical link to a follow-up meeting with the customer executive, or with an individual that he or she identifies, in order to develop or present a more specific value proposition.
- Close the meeting by expressing your appreciation for the executive's time and interest. Restate your belief that the potential exists to make a contribution to the customer's business along the lines of the value statement that you have developed.

5. Define Your Support Base Objectives

Your goal at this stage of the relationship management process is to build your support base, more specifically to develop allies and supporters who are in the Power Base, in order to build momentum within the account.

You have succeeded with your initial meeting, and hopefully are speaking with customer executives who are in the Power Base or who can help direct you into the Power Base.

The support base map, shown in Figure 5.4, is a sales tool that will assist you in anticipating future changes in the customer's internal political structure, well before the competition has any clue as to what is happening. It is a product of the Fox Evaluator and Contact Evaluator sales tools that we discussed earlier.

We have already talked about allies, supporters, and nonsupporters. Opponents are customer individuals who oppose you, not necessarily because they are aligned with the competition, but often because of internal reasons. It may be that you are dealing with an in-house group that sees you as a threat. Or, it may be a person who has had a negative experience with your company—or who supports a different company as a supplier. For example, remember our negative referral with Fred Mason, back in Sales Example 2 of Chapter 1.

Sales Example 13–Building a Support Base Map

This view of an account is very nontraditional, and that is why it has the potential to directly help you to build competitive advantage. Let's examine the following example, illustrated in Figure 5.5.

Let's assume that Bill Thomas (BT) is the executive Fox with whom you met initially. At that point he was a nonsupporter until the end of the meeting, when you felt that he had become a supporter. He was receptive to your value statement and has volunteered to involve other executives and managers in the process of further exploring how you can work together. One of those managers is George Abor (GA), who reports to Bill Thomas. George also starts off as a nonsupporter, but upon recognizing Bill's support for you, he becomes a supporter also. Over time, your relationship with George improves and develops so that he becomes an ally.

You can see from Figure 5.5 that we are tracking the progression of the relationship with the account. In the absence of a tool like this, there is no accurate way of actually measuring the effectiveness of your relationship development efforts, and therefore how much competitive advantage you are generating or losing.

 This is the view of a Selling Fox: If you can't measure it, you can't manage it.

Evaluating the Competition's Support Base

The same can be said for your competition. Odds are that they are not measuring the effectiveness of their relationship management activities. What does this mean to a Selling Fox? It suggests real opportunity for you to do what others are not doing. That is, to measure their progress and track it too, using the Fox Evaluator and Competitive Contact Evaluator™[4], shown in Table 5.4. Like the other sales tools that we have discussed, it is highly usable, producing a quick and effective measure of the competition's support base.

Using the Competitive Contact Evaluator, you can now compare the strength of the competition's support base with that of your own in

---

[4]Competitive Contact Evaluator™ is a trademark of Holden International.

Figure 5.4 **Support Base Map**

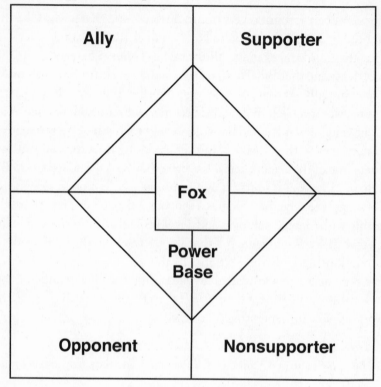

that customer company. It is a safe bet that whoever has the strongest support base will win.

If that puts the competition ahead of you, set specific objectives relative to specific customer individuals and the relationships that you want to build with them. You must always continue to actively build and manage your support base.

6. Develop Your Value Proposition

Building your support base will give you the account exposure that you need to transition from a qualitative value statement to a more quantitative value proposition through collaboration with key customer individuals. This type of collaboration is absolutely required, as the impact

Figure 5.5 **Support Base Map with Key Players**

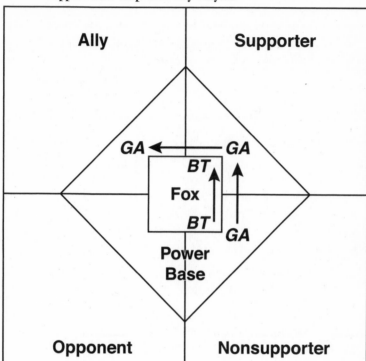

of the value proposition will only be as good as the assumptions upon which it is based. If the customer does not accept the assumptions, the proposition will fail before it is delivered.

At the same time, collaborating with the customer in this way will help you strengthen and build relationships, enhancing your support base and better positioning your company as a strategic resource to the customer. It provides balanced value, creating the important reciprocal equilibrium we discussed earlier.

7. The Value Acknowledgment Executive Meeting

Creating a formal acknowledgment at the customer executive levels relative to the value your company can provide is the seventh step in get-

Table 5.4   **Competitive Contact Evaluator**

Rate each item using the values −2 to +2. Then total your answers and use the probable results at the bottom of the page to rate the strength of your competitor's relationship with each contact.

Name of Competitor:	Competitor's Contacts (fill in contact names, one column per contact)						
−2 Almost never **−1** Rarely **0** Sometimes **+1** Often **+2** Almost always							
1. I believe my competitor is receiving support from _____, and he/she is being exposed to potential opportunities beyond the current business opportunity.							
2. _____ utilizes my competitor as a nontraditional resource through which value can be derived.							
3. _____ makes an extra effort to assist my competitor in cost-justifying the value that they can contribute.							
4. _____ introduces or references my competitor to influential people in the account.							
5. _____ has a clear strategy for establishing my competition as the preferred supplier.							
6. _____ utilizes internal contacts to provide my competition with business insights and information of a privileged nature.							
7. _____ openly discusses his/her company's plans, projects, and personnel with my competition.							

continued

Table 5.4 **Continued**

					Competitor's Contacts (fill in contact names, one column per contact)						
-2 Almost never	-1 Rarely	0 Sometimes	1 Often	+2 Almost always							
8. _____ can articulate my competition's long-term strategy for building a relationship with his/her company and how the current opportunity contributes to its advancement.											
9. _____ takes the initiative in assisting my competition in the current business development opportunity.											
10. I feel my competitor's relationship with _____ transcends the business development opportunity at hand.											
14 to 20 = Ally (A) 4 to 13 = Supporter (S) −10 to 3 = Nonsupporter (N) −20 to −11 = Opponent (O) **Totals**											

ting an executive calling process underway. It is here that you will present the preliminary value proposition for review and enhancement. Always position it as a *preliminary* value proposition, which suggests that you expect to make changes, based upon input you receive at the meeting.

Shape and refine the value proposition there with the customer; be fully prepared to explain how the value will actually be realized in terms of project implementation and results measurement. All this sets the stage for you to seek an *agreement in principle* for proceeding, which, as you will recall, is actually a trial close.

Moving beyond the presale phase of your relationship with an account and into the project implementation phase, you should continue with value acknowledgment types of executive meetings, in order to

- Report on project status and progress, conducting periodic executive briefings.
- Ensure that you receive credit at the executive levels relative to the business impact you are achieving, or have achieved, for the customer. This requires excellent and continuous tracking of results against your value proposition. That may sound simple enough, but the tendency of many salespeople is to turn their attention to the next major sales opportunity, at the expense of certainty that they have delivered on their previous commitments.

The Selling Fox's Perspective on Calling High

Everyone in sales wants to be effective in calling high, but only Selling Foxes really understand and invest in their need to grow personally in this area. They are the ones who continue to strive to become more Fox-like themselves, to better recognize other Foxes, and to gain influential supporters and allies. The following list describes how they do that:

- They work to develop new and innovative ways of creating value for customers in balance with value for themselves and their companies.
- They take the time to acquire the necessary skills and learn to use the tools that perfect the whole process.
- They use those skills and tools to build and strengthen all their executive relationships.
- Finally, by focusing on the necessary balancing of value, penetration of the Power Base, and identification of customer executive Foxes, they master the art of relationship management, which is the foundation to any competitive sales campaign or major account penetration and development effort. Without it, no amount of strategic thinking and formulation will succeed. With it, the Selling Fox's sales strategy will slice to the heart of the competition with surgical precision—a topic we address in the next chapter.

The Fox Ethos

Let's continue to build our list of Fox-like attributes, as they relate to this chapter:

The Fox Ethos

Foxes recognize other Foxes and are masters of the art of relationship management.

Foxes build support bases, knowing that whoever has the strongest support base usually wins.

Foxes are not egocentric and run silent most of the time, not seeking personal recognition or boasting about successes—they are interested only in results.

Foxes are good listeners. This is fairly easy for Selling Foxes, who focus not on themselves, but on others.

Foxes maintaining high standards of personal integrity—seeking out and aligning with others of high integrity.

Foxes are mission driven, attaching higher order purpose to anything significant, knowing well how to hook the agenda of a customer Fox for mutual advantage.

Foxes rely on measurable results, knowing that if you can't measure it, you can't manage it.

Foxes focus on balance and value, taking the long-term view toward ensuring success.

6

The King of Sales Strategy

For the past 25 years, I have worked extensively with the four classes of strategy: direct, indirect, divisional, and containment. In my experience, I have never seen a successful sales campaign that did not fall into one of those four strategy classes. We've touched upon these strategies in preceding chapters, which is a good precursor to what we are going to discuss here. Before we can begin, however, take a moment to look at how you personally sell and consider the following question:

"What do I count on to win?"

Most salespeople when asked this question tend to focus on the tangible, responding with

- My product or service
- Price/performance
- Our company's reputation
- Customer value

All of these are indeed sources of competitive advantage, but they are based upon *what* you are selling and not on *how* you are selling.

How You Sell Is Important

Here, we are interested in the *how* of your selling techniques. What we are talking about is how you manage the customer environment, which includes everything from addressing product and service issues to various business considerations, customer political factors, and philosophical concerns associated with aligning your company with that of your customer. It also means doing all of this in balance with your management of the competitive environment, where everything you do in the sales cycle is measured by how much competitive advantage it produces for you.

These concepts are explained in some depth in my previous books, but suffice it to say that strategic formulation is the domain of Selling Foxes, who count on how they sell, and not simply what they sell, to win.

People who depend on the more tangible, what they sell in order to win are largely confined to the *direct* sales strategy, which they implement again and again. Of the four classes of strategy, the direct approach is the most resource intense, requiring clear superiority to win. It is also the most predictable and therefore very vulnerable to defeat by Selling Foxes, who deploy an effective competitive counterstrategy. Rarely do salespeople who go direct consider the other classes of strategy, as their comfort zone centers on the more tangible, straight-on, generally product-focused approach to selling.

Indirect Is King

On the other hand, Selling Foxes, who depend on how versus what they are selling, know they have full operational use of all four classes of strategy. But in particular, Selling Foxes count on one class to win their most important, most competitive sales situations—the indirect strategy. In my opinion, the indirect strategy should be driving 90 percent of your wins. I consider it the king of sales strategies.

It certainly does not apply to all sales situations, but when things get hot, there is no other type of strategy that I will count on as much to win as going indirect. In fact, when I qualify a sales opportunity that I know will be highly competitive (in order to decide whether or not to pursue it), the first thing I do is evaluate it to determine whether an indirect sales strategy could be put into play. Why?

Indirect Brings Positive Qualities to Competitive Selling

Let's look at the positive qualities of the indirect strategy:

Indirect is difficult to counter from a competitive point of view. When you go indirect, your actual strategy is not as obvious, as would be the case with a direct or divisional strategy.

Indirect incorporates the element of surprise. "In battle, confrontation is done directly, victory is gained by surprise."[1] The competition may have an ability to counter your indirect strategy, but if they are not well prepared, or find themselves momentarily disoriented as to what to do, they will lose significant competitive advantage at a point when they can rarely recover in time to recoup that advantage.

Indirect works to competitive psychology. It is not uncommon for the competition, which will view itself as in the lead prior to your changing the ground rules, to develop a false sense of security and perhaps become a little complacent. This phenomenon has very real implications in terms of the competition's damaging its own response capability.

Indirect is a time-sensitive strategy. If your timing is too early, the effectiveness of your indirect approach will be compromised, as *de facto* it will become a direct strategy. Timing the shift late in the game just before a buy decision doesn't give the competition time to respond for several reasons.

- The competition often is fully committed to their existing direct approach, making it difficult for them to formulate and shift to an alternative strategy.
- If they were to attempt a shift, it would necessitate getting to new players within the account, which can be difficult with limited time, especially when the people they need to contact are predisposed to go with the competition.
- The customer buying process may not permit the delay that would be necessary in order for them to make a shift in their approach.

Indirect possesses an important loss recovery quality. If your timing in changing the ground rules is a bit too late, it can destabilize the cus-

---

[1]*The Art of War: Ancient Military Strategy for Modern Business* by Sun Tzu. Chapter 5: "Strategic Advance."

tomer's buying process and vendor evaluation, producing a positive containment effect on the sales situation. That slows everything down, providing you with the time you need to secure a customer commitment, if possible. Even if the customer has made an informal commitment to your competitor, you may still be okay if you have altered the buying criteria, negating any past decisions that took place before the new criteria were introduced. Note that without this type of new information, a customer might be hard pressed to change position on vendors—for fear it might engender a negative reflection of his or her judgment within the company. So new information that alters buying criteria is an important aspect of loss recovery, as is illustrated in Chapter 3.

Indirect is politically sensitive. Influencing the customer's buying process in a positive and constructive manner requires political strength that is only resident within the customer's organization. Therefore, your alignment with a customer Fox is extremely important when going indirect.

Indirect is a systems-oriented strategy. Unlike going direct, in which you push forward with a straight-line approach to establishing value, the indirect strategy requires that you set the stage to alter the decision-making criteria earlier in the sales cycle and then, at a right point in time, connect the dots altering the buying criteria. Each dot is part of the strategic system that you build. Think of it as a matrix, as in the following simplified example.

ᛘ Sales Example 14–The Indirect Strategy Matrix

The matrix approach to building an indirect strategy not only characterizes this type of strategy, but can also serve as an excellent sales tool to building or formulating indirect strategy. All of the critical components are included. The absence of any of these critical components would suggest that you may not be ready to go indirect. Let's look at the example illustrated in Table 6.1.

In this example, Mary is our salesperson. There are two significant buying criteria, identified in the matrix as A and B. The customer department making the purchase decision is X. Kevin, the manager of X, is weak politically, but he will make the final decision about which vendor is selected. Bob, the engineer reporting to Kevin, is technologically

Table 6.1 **Indirect Strategy Matrix**

Buying Criteria (Timing)	Customer Individual	Political Status	Personal Agenda	Connection between Criteria and Agenda
A (currently part of the evaluation)	Kevin, manager of dept. X	Not in the Power Base	Job security, but responsible for the buying decision	Will make the "safe" buy—all product capabilities must be proven
B (currently part of the evaluation)	Bob, engineer in dept. X	Not in the Power Base, but could move into it in the future	Technology-focused and would like to get out of department X	Wants the latest technology, different from his boss
C—new (will be introduced the day before the committee meets to make a decision)	Sharon, manager of dept. Y	Fox	Making her company more competitive in the marketplace through the use of new technology	c and d are state-of-the-art capabilities that will create competitive differentiation for her company
D—new (will be introduced the day before the committee meets to make a decision)	Matt, senior engineer in dept. Y	In the Power Base—friends with the engineer in dept. X	Technology-focused	Wants the latest technology and has the support of the Fox

focused. Bob is actually more aligned with Matt, the senior engineer in department Y, than he is with Kevin, his own boss in X.

Originally, the equipment being acquired was to be purchased by Kevin for department X, and would reside there. Upon realizing that with the acquisition, department X would have significantly more capacity than it needs, Mary came up with the idea of approaching Sharon, the manager of department Y, who will likely need similar capability in the future.

In preparing to connect the two sets of requirements, Mary determined that the technological strength of her solution would provide her with the competitive differentiation that she needs to win the business. She also knows that without Sharon and department Y, that strength would be of no value, given Kevin's preference for older technology that is more proven. Mary decides to get to know Sharon and discovers that she is a customer Fox.

Mary knows that the timing for bringing Sharon, department Y, and the new advanced capabilities c and d into the picture has to be just right. She concludes that just before Kevin, the manager of X, meets with his team to make the decision, she needs to be ready to go—the 11th hour will have arrived. Through her discussions with Sharon, Mary determines that Sharon will fully support her. In fact, she shares with Mary that her department will fund a good part of the acquisition, as her group will be using the equipment to support pilot production of a new, advanced product.

Politically, things will get very interesting. When Mary introduces the new interdepartmental approach and the advanced capability that will make it possible, Kevin, the manager of X, will probably delay making the final buy decision—first, in order to better understand what Mary is proposing, and second, because he knows that Sharon and department Y will most likely end up managing the installation. Only they have the resident technical expertise to program and support the equipment, tasks that would otherwise have to be outsourced if department Y were not involved. It will also mean a partial merger of X and Y departments' capital budgets, as it relates to the acquisition, further destabilizing Kevin's already weak position.

For an insecure guy like Kevin, this could mean trouble. At the same time, he cannot openly oppose the idea. It does make sense, and although he is not very astute in company politics, he does know that

Sharon, the manager of Y, is politically more powerful than he. For Kevin, this all adds up to one long, sleepless night. If he drags his feet or shows signs of opposition, he could easily fall into a power struggle with Sharon. Even if he had a good reason for doing so, he would lose, for influence flows out of the Power Base, where Sharon resides, and not into it—and it would only be bloody for Kevin to try that tactic.

Meanwhile, another sleepless night is tormenting Mary's competitor. His proven older technology and its ease of use had endeared his solution to Kevin. In fact, based on Kevin's encouragement and positive feedback, he'd been sure he had the business locked up, putting it in the 90 percent category of his sales forecast. He had already in his mind begun spending the commission and was hoping his company's high achievers club meeting would be in Hawaii again this year.

Now, upon learning of the new customer requirements, he is angry and a bit confused, but he figures that time is still in his favor. His company is working on new technology that will make his offering even more competitive than Mary's. A bit of complacency had set in, but now the competitor is unsettled and worried, and he has good reason to be. Mary has gone indirect, changing the ground rules.

Actually, if the competitor had really done his homework and had called on Sharon during the initial sales cycle, he would have learned that their requirements were *not* time sensitive, and therefore he might have pitched his pending new technology to Sharon, the more powerful manager. But not having called on her, or Matt, the senior engineer, or anyone in Y, the competitor did not know that. Instead, he had focused all his effort on the so-called decision makers in X, and being a stranger to the customer's internal politics, he was a stranger to the real Fox—Sharon, the manager of Y department.

 Only a Selling Fox will recognize and sell to a customer Fox, independent of his apparent involvement, or even lack of involvement, in a buy decision.

Still, the competition reasons, if he brings in his product development people to talk to Kevin, and they carefully sell futures, it could be enough to regain his lead just long enough to close the business. He decides to propose a migration path strategy that will lead to *c-* and *d*-type higher technology in the future, and hope that the time frames will work.

Tensions are running high, particularly when Kevin detects his own engineer Bob's enthusiasm for Mary's solution, as opposed to his. Matt, the senior engineer in Y, has set up a meeting for Mary with Bob in department X who, as it turns out, would like nothing better than to be reassigned to work with Matt in department Y, using Mary's solution.

While this strengthens Mary's support base considerably, it also causes Kevin to feel that he is now fighting not just for his department, but for his own position. Mary now represents the enemy to Kevin. This moves him more firmly into the competitor's camp. He quickly meets with the competitor to map out a plan, but it will not succeed. Why not? *Because Kevin is outside the Power Base*, which is already moving forward on this acquisition beyond Kevin's span of knowledge and control. How could that have happened? Here's how a customer Fox operates:

A day earlier, Sharon had met informally at lunch with Morris, the company CFO. In Mary's preparation to change the ground rules, she had of course produced a draft value proposition that pointed the way to significant potential positive financial impact on their business by using Mary's company's solution. Sharon had casually presented that value proposition to Morris, the CFO, during the lunch meeting. Together, and with the support of others, they made the decision to go with Mary.

Later today, a stunned Kevin will get a call from the vice president (VP) to whom he reports, complimenting him on the decision to team up with department Y on this acquisition, and for exercising good judgment in going with Mary's company's solution.

By using the indirect matrix and the value proposition to her best advantage, and unearthing Sharon, the customer Fox in department Y, Mary successfully changed the ground rules. In the 11th hour, she repositioned herself with the *real* decision-makers in the customer's organization, and through that maneuver won the business.

Indirect Has Fox-Like Qualities

Let's look at Table 6.2, which shows how the qualities of the indirect strategy compare to the operating attributes of a Fox.

It is no coincidence that going indirect is generally the approach of choice for a Selling Fox, as foxes personify the indirect strategy. Master this strategy and you will know the way of the Fox.

Table 6.2 **The Indirect Nature of a Fox**

Indirect Strategy Qualities	Fox-Like Operating Attributes
It is difficult to counter from a competitive point of view.	Foxes always determine where the high ground is, landing not just on their feet, but looking down on the opposition.
It incorporates the element of surprise.	Influence itself is not visible; only the exertion of influence can be seen. Foxes move behind the scenes, visible only when a decisive blow is in order. Even then, it can be difficult to trace it back to the Foxes.
It works to competitive psychology.	Foxes know that understanding the opposition's personality makes the opposition predictable. Conversely, Foxes generally carry great personal mystique.
It is a time-sensitive strategy.	Foxes understand time and its value. Unlike many, they make time tangible in terms of its impact on an endeavor. Quick is not necessarily better to a Fox.
It possesses a loss recovery quality.	Most people don't like to think about the negative. Foxes embrace it as a friend, knowing that the negative can become a positive.
It is politically sensitive.	The proper use of power—that is, power with purpose—is central to the existence and longevity of Foxes.
It is a strategic systems perspective.	Foxes always see the big picture. They look at all angles, thinking geometrically about all the factors involved and their relationships to one another. Foxes think from the bottom to the top, from the highest level to the lowest, and from the past to the future.

Real-Life Examples of the Indirect Strategy

In business, a hierarchy of strategy exists. A company, particularly a start-up, will normally have developed a business strategy that it is counting on to be successful. One step down, there are departmental strategies that relate to specific functions of the business. At times, the two levels join to form one corporate strategy, which is the case when a marketing strategy takes on corporate and global significance. Such was the case with Boeing Corporation.

Sales Example 15—Airbus Takes On Boeing

The Boeing-Airbus corporate duel over multibillion dollar sales for dominance over the next generation in passenger aircraft has been the subject of many articles and cover stories. One of the more notable was the cover of *Aviation Week & Space Technology*'s Report for the Paris Air Show 2001 in June. *Newsweek,* in an international edition of its magazine, has also addressed this epic battle between U.S. giant Boeing and European upstart Airbus, in articles like "Is Boeing Beating Airbus?"— and no wonder.

The aircraft business is a high-stakes game, with the U.S. corporation Boeing normally making the rules—or at least that's how it's been up to now. However, Airbus, the European answer to Boeing, achieved its first real touchdown, so to speak, against the American giant in the early 1990s, matching Boeing for global market share of new jetliner sales. At the same time, Boeing had changed its corporate strategy to focus more on diversification. As profit margins shrank in the commercial aircraft industry, Boeing looked to satellite communications and other areas in order to become a more stable and diversified conglomerate. Then Boeing made the startling announcement that it was moving its corporate headquarters, based for many years in Seattle, where Boeing builds its giant planes, to more centrally located Chicago.

Perhaps sensing vulnerability, and certainly enjoying their market share success, Airbus had driven the stakes of this heated competition to an all-new stratum—the A380. This $10 billion commitment to build a technologically advanced, superjumbo aircraft was one of the boldest moves ever in the flight industry, reminiscent of the early Concorde days, when the United States and Russia opted out of the supersonic passenger jet market.

Internally, Airbus had been gearing up for a fight. Having operated as a patchwork quilt, multinational organization consisting of German, British, Spanish, and French constituencies, company officials at Airbus apparently realized that to take on Boeing, they had to run the business as one virtually seamless company, thereby allowing Airbus to cut costs and become less dependent on government backing. The stage was set for a bet-the-farm direct strategy—bigger will certainly be better.

Initially, the Airbus strategy appeared to be working. Through aggressive marketing and attractive discounting, the company reportedly racked up 62 orders for its new jumbo passenger plane. 50 orders were reportedly written at the launch of the A380, creating an air of great optimism. Boeing appeared to be backing away from its traditional global command of the airplane design and manufacturing business, and accepting that Airbus would be the new major player in that industry. *Or was it?*

It was a shock to the industry when Boeing unleashed what appeared to be an indirect strategy. Bigger was not better. Rather, *speed* would be the success factor. Boeing changed the ground rules, going from a bigger luxury liner orientation to a faster, close-to-the-speed-of-sound solution for its customers.

Boeing apparently recognized that what travelers wanted most was more time at destinations and less time spent getting there. The Sonic Cruiser could be the answer—economical for the airline operators, time-saving for business people and leisure travelers alike, with the appeal of being a more elegant, space-age way to fly.

It probably took nanoseconds for the airline operators to assess their risk. If they committed to Airbus for the A380, and the Sonic Cruiser took off, so to speak, it could be like investing in a new class of larger, more luxurious train at just the point when air travel was about to take over, speeding people to their destinations. It could be a mistake from which a carrier might not easily recover, at least not for a long time, given the cost of the two completely opposing new designs.

Conceptually, the bet-the-farm position was then shared by the operators, a decision that each airline would have to consider carefully. That meant taking time to evaluate further before making a final buy decision. For Airbus, could that have meant time without orders being filled?

It was difficult to know. At the time of the 2001 Paris Air Show, Airbus had reportedly secured orders for 175 aircraft, a number still apparently short of what was required for the business to break even. The big unknown at the time was how many of those orders would become actual deliveries that generate actual revenue.

Offsetting this unknown might have been Airbus's entry into the high-speed market, but given its financial and organizational investment in the A380, it would have been difficult to launch a Sonic Cruiser equivalent project.

If the Boeing strategy had a containment effect on A380 orders, could it be self-sustaining in nature? It was publicized that early A380 customers enjoyed some level of discount. Given the situation, for Airbus to sell more A380s would the company have to continue discounting, which could cause customers to hold off temporarily on placing orders, hoping for a better deal?

The A380 was the hottest European technological statement in a long time, making the struggle really a battle between Europe and Boeing. But did Boeing out-strategize the competition?

Everything Boeing did spoke to an indirect strategy, but what about the timing factor? Boeing was not taking orders at that point, so how could this have been the 11th hour that so characterizes the indirect approach?

It may be that Boeing was going to change the ground rules yet again, in another way, and even later in the game. Perhaps the Sonic Cruiser's long-range ability to fly point-to-point routes, avoiding hubs and changeover delays for passengers, would prove to be a deciding factor, or perhaps other issues would surface in the future, causing size to be viewed as a liability—perhaps logistics, security. At the same time, the 777/747-series aircraft could be utilized to put further price pressure on A380 sales.

Boeing's apparently graduated strategy to change the ground rules, first to speed versus size, time versus luxury, and perhaps later to point-to-point versus hub-to-hub, might prove to be one of the best and biggest examples seen to date of the indirect approach.

Sales Example 16–Cisco: Taking On the Competition

As a sales executive, the majority of your time is most likely spent taking on competition for new sales opportunities, which is where the indirect strategy shines. An excellent example is Cisco Systems.

To say that Cisco is in the networking business is like saying that Ferrari is a car company. Sure, Cisco sells network products like switches, routers, and more, but their focus is on helping customers ". . . integrate their business goals and network strategies to implement Internet business solutions that increase productivity and improve customer care."[2] The result, according to Cisco, is:

- To lower the network's total cost of ownership
- To maximize the return on investment
- To provide seamless services enterprise-wide, enabling applications and enhancing their performance
- To better control network resources
- To speed up project implementation
- To "minimize risk and complexity."[3]

Unlike many companies, Cisco has a penchant for practicing what it preaches, applying its own technology internally and producing some impressive results:

- 90 percent of orders are taken online.
- Monthly online sales exceed $1 billion.
- $1.4 billion in financial benefits have been realized.
- 82 percent of support calls are now resolved over the Internet.
- Customer satisfaction has increased significantly.[4]

It is a strong story from a strong company that delivers strong value to customers, but that doesn't mean that Cisco is immune to market

---

[2]Cisco Systems web site. Available at [http://www.cisco.com/warp/public/779/largeent/issues/]. Retrieved mid-2001.

[3]Cisco Systems web site. Available at [http://www.cisco.com/warp/public/779/largeent/why_cisco/]. Retrieved mid-2001.

[4]Cisco Systems web site. Available at [http://www.cisco.com/warp/public/779/ibs/vertical/story/]. Retrieved mid-2001.

downturns or that it does not have competitors. On the contrary, at the product level, competition is fierce, with smaller companies offering price performance advantages that can be extremely attractive. When Cisco is brought into a sales opportunity by a network manager looking to add a router—a piece of equipment that helps a network talk to the outside world, tying into external wide area networks (WANs)—the point-to-point competition is as tough as it gets, and Cisco can lose. It is at times like this that going direct can be just too risky. Rather, the situation is made to order for the indirect sales strategy.

Bob Anderson, operations director for Cisco in Austin, Texas, talks about how Cisco changes the ground rules. As a senior sales executive with over 20 years of selling experience, Bob and others at Cisco have made a science of the indirect approach. It was a privilege for me to have the opportunity to interview Bob and to have his permission to share some of his thoughts from that interview with you here. Anderson's responses are in italics:

"Bob, when your people are involved in a highly competitive sales situation, what do you count on to win?"

"Certainly we focus on the corporate message, but if you're not speaking to the right person in the account, or if the company is not ready to embrace the network as a business asset, winning is going to be a problem."

"So how do you deal with that?"

"In both cases, where we are too low in the customer's organization or where an educational process is required to help a customer improve their business using the network, we go Fox hunting. The key is to enable a company to see how an end-to-end solution from the desktop user to other employees and to people in the outside world will strengthen their business. It is a business leader perspective, not a technical one. Talk to the wrong person and we just represent more work to him. Talk to the right person and we represent an opportunity to make internal processes easier for employees and less costly to their company, like expense reporting, managing stock options or health care administration."

"It sounds like it is all about communications."

"Right, communicating with employees, but also with customers and others. It is about creating a new and nontraditional source of competitive advantage for companies."

"I get that, but tell me how you change the ground rules."

"Depending on the account, we run what appears to be a direct competitive campaign, but quickly set the stage to change the ground rules, as you say, from a point product solution to an end-to-end enterprise network solution. We find and align with the right Fox and at the right point, late in the sales cycle, we change the focus with the help of the Fox."

"What does that do to the network manager? Does it create a problem?"

"Not usually. He is a very important player in our world, who we want to be recognized for the business value he and his operation represent to his company. We help that. It just requires some nontraditional and enterprise level thinking."

"Bob, speaking with you, I don't sense the kind of arrogance that one might expect from a key player in a company as successful as Cisco. Why is that?"

"We are only as good as our last customer, in terms of their success in utilizing our technology to enhance their business. There is just no room for ego, only results."

Earlier, I mentioned sincerity in going indirect. Bob's last comments underscore that point. If you're in some form of a solutions business, you cannot put yourself on a pedestal that creates distance from (and thereby subordinates) the customer.

Combine the right selling attitude—that of a Selling Fox—with the right selling strategy, backed by a strong tactical campaign that leans on skills like trapping, and you will be able to successfully de-install competitors in key accounts. You will also generate more than your share of business, consistently meeting your sales goals and establishing stronger credibility with top management.

✠ Sales Example 17—Oracle Takes the Lead in Customer Relationship Management (CRM)

The indirect strategy, whether it is applied to setting corporate direction, a marketing campaign, or winning a highly competitive deal, must possess one notable quality—*vision*. The ability to see clearly what is at best a blur to others is a core requirement to changing the ground rules, and there is no better example than Oracle Corporation.

A pioneer in the relational database business, Oracle figured out how to make customers' databases more valuable by enabling customers to query the data almost any way they wanted. The customer was not limited to so-called hard-wired reports, but instead had the flexibility to extract information in a way that provided relevant insight, which in turn helped to drive better decision making. But that was only the beginning.

Oracle's strength was in its technology, but its value to customers was in how customers used that technology, which led Oracle into the world of applications. Unlike other companies, however, Oracle's entry into the ERP (enterprise resource planning) business was not mainframe based, nor even client-server based, which was the futuristic, up-and-coming technology platform at the time.

Instead, Oracle looked ahead with incredible vision and saw the potential of the Internet. For five years now, their ERP applications have been running on the Internet, an architecture that is seamless, not requiring the integration of disparate software applications. Oracle refers to this as their e-Business Suite, but today it is not limited to ERP. Bringing the voice of the customer into the Suite, Oracle reengineered their ERP applications to fit seamlessly with new CRM (customer relationship management) applications. The result?—Let's listen to the Hewlett-Packard Company:

"With our rapid rate of growth, we found ourselves with seven legacy forecasting systems," says Mike Overly, CRM implementation manager at Hewlett-Packard. "Our sales reps make commitments on what they expect to bring in every month. All of that information is then rolled up to the worldwide manager, who tries to forecast with reasonable accuracy. Unfortunately, it was impossible for the manager to push a button and get an accurate forecast, or a true view of the customer. It was all done instead via word of mouth and e-mail, so it was a very disjointed process."[5]

Oracle's vision truly takes into account the customer's customer, a view that is certainly appreciated by Hewlett-Packard. Let's look at why, in their view, they selected Oracle.

"It was pretty easy to say, 'Here are the four or five strengths Oracle has over its competitors,'" says Overly. "Oracle simply outperformed in key categories such as web access and web interface. What convinced us more than anything else, however, was Oracle's vision of where this solution is headed and the technology's openness. Being able to integrate the front office with the back office was crucial. And Oracle had a three hundred sixty degree vision. Once we took all of those factors into account, it became an easy decision to make."[6]

I recently had the opportunity to spend a little time with Mike Rosser, a 10-year selling veteran with Oracle, now in the role of VP of CRM Global Strategic Sales. His is an overlay group, working with the Oracle salespeople in the CRM area. We appreciate his input and his permission to publish this interview (Rosser's responses are in italics):

"Mike, the HP example is impressive, but there is also some pretty impressive competition out there. Why did HP select Oracle?"

"There were a lot of factors, as you would guess, but the one that stands out in my mind is our ability to provide a single view of the customer. CRM companies talk about a single view, but it is based on building 'connectors' between applications that hopefully get them to talk to each other. The rub is that no one really wants to build them or, more accurately, be responsible for them. Oracle, on the other hand, connects applications at the database level, avoiding the need to integrate at the applications level, which is good for customers, bad for the integrators who sell integration projects."

"So this single view is where anyone who touches a customer, all the sales channels for example, work off one database, providing information to sales, marketing, whoever?"

[5]Oracle web site. Available at [http://www.oracle.com/corporate/strategy/index.html?success.html]. Retrieved mid-2001.

[6]Oracle web site. Available at [http://www.oracle.com/corporate/strategy/index.html?success.html]. Retrieved mid-2001.

"That's right. Our customer's customer may want to look at their invoices. Our approach enables that company to effortlessly tie into, let's say SAP[7] in the back office, to quickly get the information, the way they want to see it."

"Mike, given what you have said and the reaction of your customers, how are you changing the ground rules in this business?"

"We are doing that in a couple of ways. First, we are helping to shift legacy thinking from costly integration of applications to the seamless ease and effectiveness of the e-business suite approach, involving our own applications and those of other companies. We are waging war on complexity for all the right reasons. That's the corporate perspective."

"What about the sales perspective, what you count on to win business?"

"That's where this business really gets interesting. In the area of CRM, customer executives want information as to what their salespeople are doing, what's going on in the field, but most often it is either not provided or it is inaccurate. Some companies think that they can actually mandate or legislate it from the field, only to find out that they have damaged morale and possibly encouraged dishonesty. I won't go into the reasons for that, which center on CRM usability. My point is that you need to look at what salespeople are doing within the context of what their customers are doing. If you don't focus on the customer's customer, you miss the mark. We're changing the ground rules in sales situation after sales situation from the traditional approach of requiring salespeople to fill out forms, to new intelligent applications that provide sales guidance and direction within the context of a single view toward their customers."

"Who, within the customer's organization, do you present this approach to and at what point in the sales cycle?"

"Probably in half of the sales situations, we are finding that the CIO [chief information officer] is in tune with this thinking. He understands that his organization has the potential to become a source of business advantage for his company, producing tangible returns. Sometimes, that is not the case and we are working with senior management or heads of departments like sales or marketing. The one person who seems to always get it is the CEO. On the timing issue, we win when we involve the right players, who see the vision. To

---

[7]Systems Application Protocol.

make that vision real, we are able to map out a rapid deployment plan for a customer installation in the 11th hour of the sales situation. If we are aligned with people in the customer's Power Base, we have a very good shot at changing the ground rules and winning the business."

"Mike, if Oracle succeeds in changing the mind-set of the industry, away from integration, where will you be, as a company, in five years?"

"Our goal is clear. We want to earn the right to be the industry leader by providing our customers with simpler, faster time to performance, value-centric CRM applications that tangibly advance their businesses. We think that the winds of change are blowing."

Indirect Wins for Selling Foxes

We've just seen some real-world examples of how the indirect strategy, using changing the ground rules and other tactics, have helped some of today's industry leaders drive their business and increase sales. For the Selling Fox, we have observed how the use of the indirect strategy matrix, along with alignment with customer Foxes, helps differentiate Selling Foxes from their competitors and enables them to launch 11th-hour offensives, using the king of strategies—indirect.

The Fox Ethos

We continue our list of Fox-like attributes, as they relate to this chapter:

The Fox Ethos

Selling Foxes will recognize and sell to a customer Fox, independent of their apparent involvement, or even lack of involvement, in the buy decision.

Selling Foxes will look at every potential sales situation from bottom to top, side to side, and from every angle—thinking geometrically.

Selling Foxes work behind the scenes, gathering insight and support, launching competitive initiatives only at decisive moments.

7

De-Installing a Competitor

C loser to home is the application of the indirect strategy for displacing competition within major accounts. Businesses grow by capturing and retaining the right accounts. In selling, we know that all customers are not created equal; some represent more business value to us than others. We will refer to these as *major accounts*.

De-Installing a Competitor in a Major Account

It is our major accounts that we must protect, building immunity to competitive displacement whenever possible. Conversely, it is also our job to penetrate those same major accounts that are held just as tightly by the competition.

To accomplish this goal, we have access to three classes or types of sales strategy:

- *Direct*—taking on the competition head-to-head
- *Indirect*—creating quicksand beneath the feet of the competition in the 11th hour
- *Divisional*—inching your way into the account, one step at a time

While each of these approaches has its merits, only one is strong enough to take an account away from the competition in the shortest amount of time. I'm sure that by now you can guess which strategy that is. But first, let's look briefly at all three in light of the specific type of sales campaign we're now addressing—de-installing a competitor:

Direct: This strategy requires massive amounts of superiority, such as when the installed supplier cannot do the job for a customer with a new application, and there is no chance of that supplier's being able to perform to the new application's requirements within an acceptable time frame. Basically, the competitor just hands the account over to you—a rare occurrence. There are also times when your company will introduce new capabilities that would be very valuable to a competitively held account, but even then, successful penetration is difficult and uncertain.

Indirect: This strategy also requires strong superiority, but is different from going direct in that:

- The source of sales superiority is more customer-political than anything.
- The indirect approach often has a destabilizing effect on installed competitors, disorienting them in a somewhat predictable fashion.

Divisional: This would mean getting your foot in the door by partitioning customer requirements, through which you actually complement the installed competitor. This can look like an attractive approach and sometimes is, but more often it is attempted without the desired results. A divisional approach is a derivative of the direct strategy and as such, it is predictable and time-consuming. If the installed competitor is on top of its game, it will use that time to first contain you, then purge you from the account over time. Nevertheless, under the right circumstances, the divisional strategy can be effective.

The strategy of first choice for a Selling Fox is always the same—master the indirect approach, and you will move into competitively held accounts like a customer Fox moving throughout his or her organization. But keep in mind, timing can be everything—if and when you decide to strike.

When Should You Pursue?

Committing to the displacement of an installed competitor within an important account should be a carefully calculated decision. You will invest significant time and resources into such a campaign, so it is imperative that you know:

- This is the right account to target.
- This is the right time to launch an offensive.
- You and your company have the resources required to effect the displacement, and are willing to commit those resources.

Accomplishing this requires a more-than-casual approach to opportunity analysis, in which you often develop only a sense or feeling for whether to pursue a sales opportunity.

Here, you need to know *clearly* and *objectively* that the potential sales return from the account you are targeting for de-installation of a competitor is acceptable against the cost and effort it will require, and that the odds for a successful penetration are favorable. It is a process that begins with a business or financial analysis relative to your existing account mix and a consideration of the business potential of adding the account to that mix.

Let's assume that you, as a sales executive, are currently working on:

- *Two major accounts*, both of which represent strong repeat business potential and are strategically significant in that they provide key referrals for you—let's refer to these as Category A accounts.
- *Five competitive accounts* in which short-term active and competitive sales situations exist—let's refer to these as Category B accounts.
- *Five demand creation accounts* in which you are developing long-term opportunities in a consultative manner that will most likely not be very competitive when they mature—let's refer to these as Category C accounts.
- A *host of maintenance and very early development accounts*—let's refer to these as Category D accounts.

Suddenly, a new opportunity presents itself, but it is in a competitively held account. In the past, you would certainly have gone after the business, but with the understanding that it was a long shot. It would not go on your sales forecast, and management would understand that any win potential was low. You would fly in, size up the situation, and if you made progress, perhaps you'd get serious about pursuing it. If not, you would simply fly on to other more promising targets.

But this time is different. You sense, or have reason to believe, that penetrating this new account could be very significant for your company and that it should be pursued, but how will that impact your other accounts, which are very time-demanding? Even more important, how will you motivate your company and its management to back you with the necessary resources to get the job done? Are you even sure that it should be seriously pursued?

Every sales performer in today's marketplace faces this dilemma, but a Selling Fox addresses it with a sense of precision and process that takes the guesswork out of the equation.

Sales Example 18–Assessing Territorial Impact

The process begins with a financial assessment of your present sales territory, mapping it to determine whether it makes sense to invest in the displacement of the competitor relative to this new account. Here's the process:

First, recognize that each account category above, A through D, represents a different terrain profile in these areas:

- Cost of sales
- Sales and profit potential
- Time to closure
- Time and resource commitment

Table 7.1 illustrates how these differences map out for the sample account mix that we presented for this situation.

We focus primarily on Categories A–C, estimating in quantitative fashion:

- Cost of sales
- Your personal hit rate or sales effectiveness
- Three-year account sales potential
- Profit potential

Table 7.1 **Account Terrain Map**

	Category A	Category B	Category C	Category D
Cost of sales	High	Reasonable	Reasonable	Minimal
Sales and Profit Potential	High sales potential, acceptable profit (volume discounted)	Average deal size, good profit	Average deal size, very profitable	Too early to assess
Time to Closure	Long	Typical	Long	Too early to assess
Time and Resource Commitment	Heavy	Typical	Reasonable	Too early to assess

Examining these factors will enable us to determine the potential profit impact of any mix of account opportunities, even to approximating the earnings-per-share impact that you and your sales colleagues could have on your company's business. For example, assume that the information mapped out in Table 7.2 applies to the two A accounts, five B accounts and five C accounts.

Cost of sales includes the cost of labor (loaded compensation), travel, support resources, development, and other expenses that are necessary to develop the account or sale.

Sales hit rate represents the average percentage of sales wins to total orders pursued, generally determined over the preceding year.

3-year sales potential per account takes into consideration the dollar size of transactions and the potential for repeat business over a three-year period, which in today's changing markets is a reasonable time horizon.

Profit potential per account is a function of:

- Cost of sales
- The dollar amount of services or other high-margin offerings that are bundled into a sale to create a more effective solution to meeting the customer's needs

- Applicable volume discounts
- The actual margins of the products or services being sold
- Any other costs, such as third-party partnering fees, sales finders-fees, or other appropriate considerations that impact margin.

Total category profit potential adjusted for hit rate over 3 years, given the current category mix and number of accounts per category, is a number representing the profit contribution that you expect to make to your company over the three-year period.

Total category sales potential adjusted for hit rate over 3 years, given the current category mix and number of accounts per category, is a number representing the revenue contribution that you expect to make to your company over the three year period.

The territorial business impact map shown in Table 7.2 is merely a

Table 7.2 **Territorial Business Impact Map**

	Category A	Category B	Category C	Category D
Cost of sales	$100K	$20K	$25K	$5K
Sales Hit Rate	50%	40%	60%	Too early to assess
3-year Sales Potential per Account	$3 million	$500K	$500K	Too early to assess
Profit Potential per Account	$600K (20% of sales)	$125K (25% of sales)	$150K (30% of sales)	Too early to assess
Total Category Profit Potential Adjusted for Hit Rate Over 3 Years	$600K	$250K	$450K	Too early to assess
Total Category Sales Potential Adjusted for Hit Rate Over 3 Years	$3 million	$1 million	$1.5 million	Too early to assess

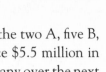

snapshot in time. In this case, suggesting that if only the two A, five B, and five C accounts were pursued, you would produce $5.5 million in sales, representing $1.3 million in profit for your company over the next three years. The map also reveals that one A account produces more revenue and almost as much profit to your company as all ten B and C accounts together. This is not to discount the importance of B and C accounts, as they

- Offset the often long sales cycles of category A accounts
- Buffer the impact of an A account loss
- May become A accounts over time

However, it does say that if your early development stage work in category D produces more category A accounts, your sales will grow disproportionately to the number of accounts. At the same time, these A accounts require heavy investment, which could compromise your B and C account sales activities. Therefore, the question becomes the following: Given your personal sales capacity, when should or could you pursue a new A account, taking into consideration your current mix of business? Let's assume the answer is "now," and that it would not be possible or advisable to transfer any of your A, B, or C accounts to another salesperson.

Independent of the sales worthiness of the new A account, which is a subject that we very thoroughly address in Chapter 8, if pursuing A is competitively demanding, you will compromise your current mix of business. This will manifest itself in a reduction of hit rate, most likely not in your B accounts, but in your C accounts, in which you are not under fire to close business. Going back to the territorial business impact map shown in Table 7.3, we can see the potential impact.

In my experience, the impact map reflects a conservative view of the potential negative impact, suggesting that you may lose $1 million in sales revenue and $300K in profits over the next three years by pursuing the new A account. Again, this assumes there will be no adverse impact on your B account competitive sales situations.

Although this might dissuade you from targeting new A accounts, it is not necessarily bad news. The key is to update your overall territory plan to include the potential downside and show:

- How you will make up for lost revenue as an offset, perhaps from the new A account.
- How additional sales support resources could extend your capacity, mitigating the projected downside potential.
- That all accounts that you are pursuing are in fact qualified, in terms of the quality of the business and your ability to win the business. (Note: Accounts that are not qualified or that are marginal should, in most cases, be dropped.)
- How transferring certain accounts to other salespeople could extend your coverage ability and increase, rather than risk, revenues.

Table 7.3 Potential Business Impact of Pursuing a New "A" Account

	Category A	Category B	Category C	Category D
Cost of sales	$100K	$20K	$25K	$5K
Sales Hit Rate	50%	40%	60% drops to 20%	Too early to assess
3-year Sales Potential per Account	$3 million	$500K	$500K	Too early to assess
Profit Potential per Account	$600K (20% of sales)	$125K (25% of sales)	$150K (30% of sales)	Too early to assess
Total Category Profit Potential Adjusted for Hit Rate Over 3 Years	$600K	$250K	$450K drops to $150K	Too early to assess
Total Category Sales Potential Adjusted for Hit Rate Over 3 Years	$3 million	$1 million	$1.5 million drops to $500K	Too early to assess

The problem is that most sales executives do not do this kind of analysis, exposing themselves to:

- Possible lost sales compounded by a lack of management understanding about the business trade-offs being made. This can cause unnecessary criticism and even career damage.
- Loss of the opportunity to better build their territory and increase sales by involving their management in a business analysis that (1) either takes them off the hook in redirecting their sales efforts to the A account (which is then viewed as a high priority by management), or (2) provides the necessary resources to pursue all A, B, and C opportunities.

The point here is that an overall plan for pursuit of a business-affecting case must be put in front of your management.

When it comes to de-installing a competitor in a major account, a Selling Fox always puts a business case analysis ahead of the penetration campaign, always making good overall business decisions before making specific sales opportunity pursuit decisions.

The Green Light

Let's assume that you have put your plan before management, and they have decided it is good business to go after the new A account at this time. Backing up that decision, they have provided you with the necessary sales support resources to carry forward all existing A, B, and C account efforts. If all goes to plan, these resources will free you up to launch an offensive into the new A account without significant territorial compromise. Your focus now shifts to the new account, which we will call New A. You are ready to plan your first launch to de-install the competition.

New A is, and has been for some time, a competitively held account. Penetrating it will not be easy, but with the right indirect strategy implemented at the right time, it can be accomplished. This is not to be arrogant or overconfident, as a Selling Fox is neither of these. It is simply a matter of strategic focus combined with good implementation. The issue at this stage of the penetration effort is not the competition, but rather the customer:

- Does the potential exist to provide the kind of value that will be necessary?
- Can you identify, and begin aligning with, the right Fox early enough in time to profile the account effectively and build the necessary value messaging?

As with any competitively held account, you need an inroad, and that usually is a contact—someone who will provide you with the customer information necessary to begin the executive calling process discussed in Chapter 5, the seven basic points of which are, as you'll recall:

1. Preparing for contact
2. Executive preconditioning
3. Making contact
4. The initial executive meeting
5. Defining your support base objectives
6. Developing your value proposition
7. The value acknowledgment executive meeting

The goal is to identify and get to a Fox in the customer organization as quickly as possible. There are many sources of account information, but the best insight will come from people in the Power Base. Treat those people as executives, independent of their level of authority, and apply the executive calling process in meeting with them.

Build an Account Profile

In parallel, you will want to build an account profile along the following lines:

- Analyze and succinctly describe the customer's business, core offerings, management philosophy, and operating style.

- Map out the organization chart, paying particular attention to the Power Base—look not only at corporate headquarters, but at all the appropriate business units.
- Start building your support base map for the account, which again assesses customer individuals in terms of their influence and advocacy.
- Determine where the competition is installed and identify who supports them within the customer's organization. Map those individuals to the Power Base, determining whether they are in or out.
- Describe New A's industry, the markets it serves, and its market positioning, along with present and emerging industry trends—begin to think about how those trends will or could impact New A's business.
- Identify, study, and try to understand who New A's biggest competitors are, how they differ from one another, plus how each is positioned in the marketplace compared with New A.
- Develop a sense for New A's business direction, its key initiatives, and the challenges it faces both as a company and by each division.

This profile should be narrow in its scope. It is not intended to be a comprehensive or all-inclusive description of the account. Rather, it should only contain information that is necessary to support your implementation of the executive calling process. It can always be expanded later if necessary.

Develop a Pre-Penetration Checklist

As you begin to build your list of potential key contacts in the account, you will also want to pay particular attention to several additional areas that will be surgically significant in the formation of your indirect strategy.

- Can you establish a compelling value statement with reciprocating value to your company? Will it support your getting to a Fox?
- How will the value statement lead to a value proposition and will there be a means to measure tangible results? Can you hook into a corporate initiative that will produce disproportionate value to New A?

- Who is the right Fox to be dealing with and what is his or her personal agenda and personal operating philosophy? Is alignment possible?
- To what extent do power plays or power struggles exist within New A? Does an alignment opportunity exist with a new Fox?
- What has been your company's history with New A, if any? Is that history an asset or liability to your efforts?

At the end of the process, your information should confirm both of the following:

- *This is the right account to target.*
- *This is the right time to launch an offensive.*

These two issues should be independently reconfirmed irrespective of the "yes" decision your management has just made. Propitious niche targeting and timing is critical to success in launching an offensive like this.

As you build the New A profile and work through the pre-penetration checklist, if you are able to answer all of the appropriate questions in the affirmative and confirm the final two, it is time to broaden your focus to include examination of the competition. Specifically, how you will accomplish their future displacement utilizing the indirect strategy.

Sales Example 19–Applying the Indirect Strategy

Many factors contribute to a successful displacement effort, but only three are absolutely critical. They form a *penetration triad*, around which many other important considerations exist, but they are the heart and soul of success in such a campaign as it is contemplated here. They are:

- Political alignment
- Timing
- A predictable competitive response

Keep these factors in mind as we move through the following example involving displacing the competition in New A. On everything else, you can make mistakes and recover, but in the aforementioned three areas, there is no room for miscalculation or error. To ensure that such a level of precision is achieved, use the indirect strategy matrix (Table 6.1) discussed in Chapter 6.

Living in the Rearview Mirror

As we mentioned earlier, the competition is well installed within New A, and has been for some time. It has a strong support base and understands the customer's business fairly well. Most salespeople in your position would likely put their focus on the future, looking for a new sales opportunity, a new battleground; you, however, will do the opposite. For you, it is going to be life in the rearview mirror, at least for a while. Any customer meeting that you have, any profiling, or any other customer activity you analyze will carry with it one purpose—to map out the appropriate Power Base and identify any possible power struggles or power plays.

The reason I say you'll be living in the rearview mirror is that the key to this insight resides in the past. Therefore, you'll need to determine:

- What major decisions have been made and by whom, whether they are regarding capital acquisitions, other major initiatives, or policy shifts?
- Did anyone oppose them, and if so, who? What is their position in New A, and what was the outcome?
- Where and when in any of these processes has specific personal influence been exerted?
- By whom was the influence exerted and why? You need to know where the power is.
- How did the competition tap that power?
- With whom did your competitor align, and when?

You can anticipate that the competition in this situation will respond to your indirect strategy with a direct approach. Your competitor is the incumbent and has superiority. Your job now is to establish a low profile, avoiding any temptation to present yourself openly as a threat. Keeping low visibility will enable you to quietly acquire the necessary profile information on the account. Alerting the competition to your presence too early would be counter to your ultimate intent.

Identifying Political Opportunity

Let's say that as you develop insight into the account and its history, you discover that the competition had aligned with a Fox some time ago, and has strong executive contacts. These competitive supporters will be a problem, blocking any chance for success until and unless the political landscape changes. The key is to position yourself close enough to the account to recognize and capitalize on new political opportunity, which may present itself in one of the following two forms:

- A new Fox comes onto the scene, with whom you can quickly align.
- A new or existing power struggle is identified between someone with whom the competition is aligned and a new or existing player.

Both cases usually result from an organizational change that has strong political implications. In part, this is why, as we emphasized earlier, the right timing in launching your offensive is so important.

🦊 *To make an overt move prior to aligning yourself with a new Fox, or with the individual on the winning side of a power struggle, would be sheer suicide.*

Let's assume that a new Fox emerges. You quickly evaluate the Fox, and with help from the contacts you've developed in the account, on an informal basis you bring into relief the new Fox's personal agenda. You analyze that and realize that it will likely support a shift away from the installed competitor, but only if you can provide sufficient value to help solidify the new Fox's power within New A, and also help advance his or her personal agenda as to organizational or political aspirations.

Keep in mind that this is not a time when the new Fox can afford to make a tactical mistake, so there could be a significant dependency factor characterizing the relationship, underscoring much of what is discussed in Chapter 5 concerning a Fox's principles and values. A review of that chapter and the sales tools presented there would be appropriate at this point in your approach.

Searching for a Penetration Opportunity

Next, you need an opportunity to maneuver into position, as your focus now swings from the past and the rearview mirror to studying the layout of the track to success and to the future. You need to be able to offer New A, via the new Fox, a very strong value statement or proposition based upon a new application or sales opportunity.

Shifting from the incumbent competitor to your company will no doubt cause New A to experience some conversion expense. That expense must be offset by your value proposition. If such an opportunity does not exist, then the timing for launch is not yet right. The window of opportunity is still closed. Furthermore, it needs to be an opportunity that carries with it a clear driving mechanism that frames up or bounds the sales cycle. A *driving mechanism* is some reason or event that will cause the customer to make the buy decision by a specific point in time. This becomes very important in setting the timing for your indirect strategy—changing the ground rules at just the right moment, as determined by the driving mechanism. In the case of New A, we will assume that a penetration opportunity does exist.

Penetration Timing

With these considerations in mind, proper timing to displace a competitor is set by:

- Establishing the correct political alignment
- The presence of a strong opportunity, in terms of the value you can provide
- The existence of a driving mechanism

In the background is the competition. Having worked with the customer for a long time, it is not uncommon for the competitive salesperson to be in a maintenance mode. Not sensing any competitive threat on the horizon, coupled with being under pressure to make quota, often causes salespeople to shift some of their focus to other accounts and give attention to more active or demanding sales situations. Our intent is to challenge the competition when they least expect it.

Keep in mind, however, that if the competitive salesperson is a Selling Fox, he or she will not be asleep at the switch, but will be on the lookout for competitive problems and reasonably prepared for your or anyone else's offensive. If this is the case, you will know it very soon, as serious roadblocks will pop up before your eyes. At that point, it would be appropriate to review your penetration plans, perhaps deciding not to pursue the account further. Fortunately, in one sense, Selling Foxes are still pretty rare, so it will most likely not become an issue. Let's assume that your competitor is not a Selling Fox and continue the campaign.

Find a Problem

Look for any signs of customer dissatisfaction with your competitor. In a major account environment, it is not uncommon for customer individuals to become quite focused not on the value the competitor is providing, but on its shortcomings. They have developed a dependency on the competitor, and although a lot of good work has no doubt been done, it is easy for a customer to become overly focused on problems, losing proper perspective; this generally manifests itself in the customer's perception that the supplier is being nonresponsive or insensitive to the company's needs and demands. That perception will become an important element in your penetration efforts at New A.

The action begins when the New A Fox agrees to provide you with an opportunity to prove that your company can provide quantifiable value to his or her company. Such an opportunity may be an order or a serious indication that he or she is considering the placement of an order with you. Either way, it is good news, which could cause you to feel that the penetration effort is going quite smoothly—and it is, but take a moment to understand what may be happening behind the scenes.

What is motivating the Fox? Assume that the Fox is aware that his or her company is dependent on your competitor and is somewhat unhappy with the performance of the equipment or the competitor's service and support. The customer is feeling a bit unappreciated but has not succeeded in rectifying the situation. Now comes a new New A Fox onto the scene. This Fox's plan is to strike fear into the heart of the supplier, elevating its performance, or else replacing it. If anything is going to light such a fire, it is the presence of competitive equipment—yours.

How do you feel your competitor will react? They'll hear the wake-up call. History, in general, tells us that they will quickly bring in the big guns. Their executive management will renew their commitment to the account, promise to clean up any problems that exist, and will probably even renegotiate pricing. It will be a full court press, and who do you suppose will get credit for it? Right! The new Fox, who did what others could not do—get the supplier to snap to attention by sensing the threat of a competitor—*you*. The Fox thereby places himself or herself in a win-win position:

- If your solution is successful, he or she wins and gains even more future leverage internally.
- If your solution does not produce the expected value, the new Fox still wins, having generated disproportionate value for himself or herself by lighting a fire under the feet of your competitor.

Where Does That Leave You?

This is the kind of situation in which you must constantly think like a Fox and use Fox-like tactics. It is not at all uncommon for customers to bring in new equipment on consignment, in this case possibly yours, when they can simply return it when the desired result has been achieved. Such an action allows them to protect the credibility of the installed competitors' salespeople, upon whom they are dependent for future service and support. A salesperson in such a situation becomes someone who will never forget what might happen if there are future slip-ups.

Using such tactics can be very effective, but it will likely damage the relationship of mutual trust between the customer and the installed supplier. That damage will need to be repaired, and the person responsible for doing that is the new customer Fox. It is one thing to win an order, another to accomplish an effective loss recovery effort, snatching an account back from the threat of competition. Such actions make heroes of salespeople, enhancing their influence within their own organizations, thereby increasing their ability to get things done for customers. Such must be the outcome for the competitor. To win the battle and grow in strength, the Fox must protect the credibility of the competitive salesperson.

At the same time, it is tempting for any salesperson looking to penetrate an account to agree with a customer consignment deal. It can be viewed as a foot in the door, which might be more than any other salesperson has achieved so far in trying to penetrate the account, and may even be a chance to demonstrate value, but it is fraught with risk.

Sometimes simply the customer threat to shift away from the incumbent is enough to cause the desired competitive reaction, but it is often a reaction that is predictable, causing significant competitive vulnerability for the incumbent. Exploiting that vulnerability, rather than lending equipment, will be key to the success of your indirect strategy.

New A's Fox has brought you into the account as a threat to the incumbent for a reason, which no doubt centers on your value proposition. You have delineated to the Fox some value that you can provide, which the incumbent cannot or will not provide. Possibly it is product value. However, unless the competition voluntarily abdicates its position in the account, which is highly unlikely, you cannot depend on product value alone to win the day.

 Product or service value is important, but it is not part of the aforementioned penetration triad of critical factors: (1) political alignment, (2) timing, and (3) a predictable competitive response.

Your strategy, in terms of what you are counting on to penetrate the account, must not be focused on what you are selling, but on the Fox, his or her personal agenda, and what you represent as a company. After you have those alignments, the timing is right to set a trap for the competition. The trap is what will complete the de-installment of the competitor in New A. Basically it will be a self-destruct mechanism for your competitor.

Trapping the Competition

One of your most significant tactical efforts in setting the stage to change the ground rules will be accomplished through trapping. It is imperative that you precondition everyone who is receptive within the account, including those around the Fox, to what you expect the competition will do and the significance of that to the customer, keeping in mind the Fox's personal agenda. Remember that it's an informal educational process, *not* negative selling, so take care not to cross the line that is discussed in Chapter 3. What you need to get across to the customer is:

- You know what the competition is going to do in renewing its commitment to the account, but what about its true motivation?
- Why is the competition suddenly throwing people and resources at New A? Clearly, it is to keep the account, but what does that say about the company?

What Is the Best Way to Handle This?

Your approach to the new Fox, whom we will call Alan, needs to be along the lines of what you will hear Mary, our salesperson, say in this dialog:

"Alan, we have been working together for a little while now and I think that you have developed a feeling for the type of company we are and how we operate. We have established that we can potentially provide significant value to New A in a way that I believe really differentiates us from the competition. If we end up working together in any kind of significant way, New A will certainly become somewhat dependent on us as a company, too. I say that because the level of responsiveness that you see from us now is indicative of what you can continue to expect to receive later. You will not find us becoming complacent or unresponsive, where you have to put a gun to our head in order to get the support you want and deserve. Our company is committed to doing the right things for the right reasons. We believe in helping our customers achieve their goals and we support them fully in whatever they need to make that happen."

"I appreciate that," responds the Fox. "This is hard on everyone. It is unfortunate that it is necessary."

"I agree, and you know, Alan, suppose we were the competition, and we woke up and did everything that you and New A need now—what about the future? Would we go back to the same old pattern of operating? What would have changed to suggest that we were suddenly a different company, in terms of how we treat our customers? What if your dependency on us grows? Would you have to put a bigger gun to our heads in the future—a .357 Magnum?"

"That's an unsettling question, Mary. I hadn't really thought about that aspect of the relationship. Surely, any company would say that we have nothing to fear, but you know I'm not sure. In spite of good intentions, you might be right. We could just find ourselves back where we are today."

"Our commitment to you, Alan, is that with us, that will never happen."

Sales Analysis: Reinforce the Psychological Aspects

1. You can see the logic. We are doing no more than intellectualizing what is actually happening, to ensure that New A sees the present situation with the competitor for what it really is. The intent is to educate the customer and reinforce the current situation, so that when the competition intensifies its commitment to the account, the customer is equipped with thoughtful and penetrating questions that the competition will not expect. When asked, these questions also tend to make the customer individual asking them look very intelligent and insightful.

2. You can see the approach. Mary put herself in the shoes of the competition at one point. This goes back to our earlier comment about not being too negative relative to the competition—not crossing the line. By doing this, Selling Foxes give themselves license to educate the customer more directly on the realities of anticipated competitive activities without crossing the line and engaging in negative selling themselves. In racing, we refer to this as driving to the edge, or 10-10 driving. Admittedly, it is an advanced selling technique, not without risk and not for the new salesperson, but for a Selling Fox, it is being in the zone, so to speak, where your selling or driving is strong, effective, and exhilarating.

Sales dialog (continued): This is how the conversation between New A and the competition might go down. The scene is one in which the competitive salesperson, Bill, and his VP of sales are meeting with Alan, our new Fox, and George, Alan's immediate subordinate. George is also in the Power Base, and Mary has cultivated a supporter relationship with George.

Competitive VP opens the dialog.

"Thank you, Alan and George, for taking the time to see us this afternoon. We understand that you are considering a competitive alternative for a new application here at New A and that you have not been happy with our sup-

port and responsiveness, as you and Bill have discussed. We would like to explain what we are doing to rectify the situation and to ensure that it does not occur again."

Bill and the VP go on to commit on-site support resources, free software, and a discount on future equipment. It is impressive and, for a moment, it has Alan thinking that he might stay with the supplier. Then George, with whom Mary has also spent time to set the stage for trapping the competition, speaks up.

"We certainly appreciate the strength of these commitments, Bill, and they are impressive, but I have to wonder why it took you so long to make them. I mean, you and your company knew before this that we were experiencing problems with your previous installation, right?"

"Well yes, we did, but I think we, or I, underestimated their severity."

"You mean that they became severe to you only when you thought that you might lose the account?"

At this point Bill doesn't know how to respond. He is caught in the trap. An uncomfortable silence falls in the room. Alan and George wait quietly for the supplier's response.

The competitive VP speaks up, trying to rescue Bill.

"I believe that we did let you down, Alan, but I do feel that your people at New A need to take some responsibility as well for this. We feel that some of the difficulties relate to your people who have not been capable or willing to work with us."

The VP has made the worst tactical blunder. He has shifted some of the blame to the customer. Beginning to see the handwriting on the wall, Bill shifts in his seat, visibly uncomfortable. He does not know Alan well, but he knows that this cannot possibly end up in a good place for him, and he is right about that. Alan sees immediately that the competitor lacks integrity as a company and now believes that further dependency on that company could be risky for New A. However, he does not confront them further, as there is no point in doing so. He has already learned what he needed to know. George, on the other hand, is less reserved.

"So you think that we have brought these problems upon ourselves? Incredible . . ."

Alan stops George from continuing and brings the meeting to a close.

Sales Analysis: Installed Competitor Traps Self and Loses

Sensitizing Alan, George, and others to the true motivation and operating style of the competitor has worked. As the incumbent, the competitor had the benefit of the doubt, but in that one meeting, they overreacted and blew their credibility.

 That is the strength of trapping—you lay the trap, but you don't actually trap competitors, as they will trap themselves!

The meeting will also have significance in another way. Alan's apparently unilateral decision to depart from the competitor will be met with questions by others in New A, as you might expect. Everyone will have an opinion about with whom New A should be working in the future, but Alan's influence and prior success enables him to respond to such issues with ease. He will simply say that the two companies have evolved different operating styles and priorities, making them no longer as compatible as they once were. He will emphasize that in today's volatile marketplace, he needs a supplier that will extend itself as a partner, and not just answer the need for support when new revenue from further sales hangs in the balance. Life is too short, he will emphasize, and New A has neither the time nor the inclination to continue to do business that way. As a new Fox, he will not be challenged.

What If You Are Competing with a Selling Fox?

Earlier, I mentioned that if the competitive salesperson (e.g., Bill) was a Selling Fox, you would be in big trouble trying to oust him from the customer's favor. Well, as it turns out in this example, which is based on an actual sales situation, Bill was not a Selling Fox at all. His VP was not a Fox, either.

But let's suppose Bill was a Fox. What would he have done?

A Fox-Like Approach to Loss Recovery

Certainly a Selling Fox would never have ignored the account to the extent that allowed his or her company to get into such a predicament with a competitor. But let's assume that Bill, as a Selling Fox, had just inherited the account and the situation had already developed. Expanding on our discussion of loss recovery in Chapter 4, what would he do? He would move with lightning speed into loss recovery.

There is a lot that a Selling Fox might do differently from the way Bill originally handled the situation, but one tactic that would clearly label him a Selling Fox would be to *no-bid* the new business at New A, electing not to pursue it.

That may sound almost heretical to a salesperson, but it is a significant Fox-like loss recovery tactic that can work well in a scenario like this. In a discussion with Alan, Bill's approach might go like this.

"Alan, as you know I am fairly new to the account, and have had my hands full dealing with the issues that need to be corrected here. I am still trying to get to the bottom of how New A fell off our radar screen, but everything that I know about our company tells me that this is an anomaly and not indicative of what you should have received in support, or can expect from us in the future. At the same time, I don't expect you to take that on face value. If I were you, I would not either. The only way that I can demonstrate that we are who we say we are, is to no-bid this new application. If we were to pursue that business, you would not be able to know our true motivation, which is to help make you successful for the right reasons."

"That's pretty surprising, Bill. How does your management feel about it? Do they support your position?" Alan might ask.

"Yes, and they are prepared to accept full responsibility for the problems, and to act with me to correct them as soon as possible. Only when we have reinstated ourselves in your eyes and regained your trust that we as a company care about New A's success, and you believe that we will be totally attentive to your support needs, will we consider bidding new applications."

No-bidding business really takes guts. In some companies, it is not even a possibility, as management would never approve it. Still, it is one of the most powerful support statements a salesperson can make to a customer to effect loss recovery. Interestingly, when a Selling Fox takes this kind of approach, he or she more often than not wins the new business anyway. When executed with real sincerity, it can have such a positive impact on customers that they hold off on selecting a competitor. It is a joy to observe.

In the competitive displacement sales situation illustrated, there was, however, no successful loss recovery by the installed supplier, and Mary, the Selling Fox for the new company, won the New A account and business. The effort reflected an organized deployment of the indirect strategy as part of an overall de-installation process that includes:

- Conducting a financial assessment as to the territorial impact of pursuing the de-installation of a competitor within a major account—building the business case
- Framing up a compelling value statement, along with achieving the political alignment necessary to wage the competitive campaign—positioning yourself in terms of value and influence
- Implementing the seven-step executive calling process—securing executive sponsorship
- Building an account profile—identifying what you don't know about the account
- Running a pre-penetration checklist—questions that verify that this is the right account and the right time to launch the offensive
- Formulating the appropriate indirect strategy—using the indirect strategy matrix to ensure that the penetration triad is in place
- Managing the timing of the strategic thrust—checking for a driving mechanism
- Trapping the competition—predicting competitive responses and educating the customer as to how to deal with them, in a manner that causes the competition to damage its own credibility
- Securing the first order—safely displacing the competition

That is the road map to de-installing a competitor.

The Fox Ethos

Again, let's add to our list of Fox-like attributes, as they relate to this chapter:

The Fox Ethos

Foxes think first and act second, always creating a plan using the de-installation process to ensure the successful displacement of a competitor.

Foxes are very proactive, anticipating the competition and laying traps that cause competitors to damage their own credibility.

8
Qualifying Opportunities

We have talked about the need to do an analysis of your existing business before launching a sales campaign to de-install a competitor within a major account. The business merits of that analysis took into consideration the salesperson's existing territory, which we viewed as being made up of categories A, B, C, and D accounts. It recognized that a de-installation campaign is very labor intensive and could easily impact the salesperson's competitive position in his or her existing accounts. This type of opportunity cost will always be an issue requiring careful management, but in general, qualifying a new opportunity does not need to be a complex or difficult process. It will take some time and effort in the beginning, as you develop familiarity with the process, but will soon become intuitive as you work with it.

The Opportunity Evaluator

An advanced selling tool that will assist you is the *opportunity evaluator*. Less specialized than the approach that we took to de-installing a competitor, its purpose is to aid in quickly and objectively determining whether it makes sense to go after a specific sales opportunity. To accomplish this goal, the opportunity evaluator addresses four simple operative questions:

- *Can we add value?* This helps you to quantify the reality and significance of the value that you might provide to the customer.
- *Should we pursue?* Here you are able to determine the quality of the business that you might generate with the customer, reflecting the customer's business significance to you and your company.
- *Can we compete?* This measures your competitive strength going into the sales opportunity, based upon factors that are largely *out* of your control.
- *Are we aligned to win?* This takes the process a step further, measuring your competitive horsepower, based upon factors that are largely *in* your control.

Recognizing that most salespeople are responsible for a mix of accounts and opportunities that range from large, big-ticket sales with relatively long sales cycles to those that are smaller, more transaction-driven, short-cycle deals, we will divide our discussion to focus on two types of the opportunity evaluator, *the major opportunity evaluator* and the *short-cycle opportunity evaluator.* The latter will support rapid deployment of the concepts and techniques put forth in this chapter.

We now take you step by step through the process of using them, with coaching questions to assist you in determining what you need to know in order to properly evaluate a new sales opportunity.

Major Opportunity Evaluator

This tool walks you through a four-phase process, each phase addressing a very telling question that you must answer about a new sales opportunity. The first two segments, *Can we add value?* and *Should we pursue?* are about the potential to create balanced value as discussed in Chapter 5. In fact, you may recall the balanced value principle:

 Every value contribution made or proposed should have a reciprocating component to maintain approximate equilibrium in the relationship.

This becomes very important. In addition to the scoring on the Can we add value? and Should we pursue? metrics, you need to determine

Table 8.1 **Major Opportunity Evaluator I: Can We Add Value? Metrics Chart**

Criteria	Scale		Your Scores
1. Customer Involvement in Value Discovery	+3: Proactive 0: Receptive	−3: Passive −4: Unknown	
2. Driving Mechanism	+4: Clear/Urgent 0: Clear	−3: Unclear −4: Unknown	
3. Business Impact	+4: Mission critical 0: Promising	−3: Minimal −4: Unknown	
4. Measurability	+3: Trackable 0: Accessible	−3: Problematic −4: Unknown	

Scoring Key:
- ❏ +7 to +14: **Solid**
- ❏ −1 to +6: **Emerging**
- ❏ −8 to −2: **Weak**
- ❏ −16 to −9: **Nonexistent**

whether the appropriate balance exists between the two companies for a major opportunity feasibility.

Let's look at each of the four major opportunity evaluation phases and the metrics that support them. As with all the sales tools that we discuss, it is recommended that you calibrate the opportunity evaluator tools, using live sales situations that are well known to you. Always set the scoring range by bounding both ends of the scoring continuum. In the case of the Can we add value? metric, shown in Table 8.1, select an existing sales opportunity in which you know that the value you are providing is solid, along with one in which the value is nonexistent. Adjust the scoring ranges to fit or reflect your selling environment.

In this first phase of the process, you are dealing with four criteria that measure the amount and realness of the value you might provide to a customer. Let's examine each of them, along with a number of coaching questions that will help you determine or interpret your position on each.

1. **Customer involvement in value discovery:** Actions speak louder than words. The more the customer is actively involved in the

definition and realization of the value that you believe you can create for them, the more committed that customer will be, enhancing the results.

Scoring definitions:
Proactive (+3)—This is the best case. The customer is taking some ownership of the effort, clearly recognizing the potential value that you and your company represent.
Receptive (0)—This is an acknowledgment of potential. The customer sees the possibilities only and not the value itself. For them, it is of exploratory interest.
Passive (–3)—Here, the customer does not even see potential. The customer is polite and listens, not ruling anything out, but not getting behind the effort either.
Unknown (–4)—You are unable to rank this criterion.

Coaching questions:
The best way to assess the customer and correct score is through personal observation, but you may need to take it a step further. Here is a series of questions that will help with the thought process for this criterion:

- Is the customer simply window shopping, so to speak, with no real buying motivation?
- Does the customer seem to have a predisposition, one way or the other, to do business with your company?
- Is the customer sufficiently knowledgeable to make a meaningful contribution or decision regarding value?
- Does the customer expect to be handed the answers, as opposed to being involved as part of a solutions-focused team?
- Do you have the tendency to preform opinions without proper exploration as to the value you could provide?
- Does the language of the value statement or proposition represent your company's thinking, or that of the customer, integrated with your own?

2. **Driving mechanism:** This is an impending event or action that sets a specific time frame. It may be the date that a new product will go

into production or when a company is moving its office location. It is any event that bounds the sales cycle as to when the customer must make a buy decision. Sometimes it is not an event, but an action, like the edict of a Fox who has stated that an installation must be up and running by a certain point in time.

Scoring definitions:
Clear and urgent (+4)—This is the best case. The project is considered a customer priority, with management support and a clear sense of urgency that is recognized by all involved.
Clear (0)—This is not considered an organizational priority. Here, the link between the driving mechanism and what you are proposing is not clear, but there is a driving mechanism present.
Unclear (–3)—The driving mechanism is absent or not understood. In either case, there is no real sense of urgency.
Unknown (–4)—You are unable to rank this criterion.

Coaching questions:
As before, the following questions will help with the thought process for rating this criterion:

- Is the customer pushing your company to get things going?
- Why is the timing of the customer application important?
- Is there a time-related financial consideration from the customer's viewpoint?
- Is there a time-related political consideration, perhaps involving a Fox or someone in the Power Base?
- Is customer senior management aware of the driving mechanism and its connection to your proposal?
- Is it possible to draw a line from your offering to the customer's customer or to industry trends that are impacting the customer?

3. Business impact: This is the significance of your value statement or proposition. This criterion reflects the level of customer-perceived importance to your offering or solution, based upon how it will impact their business.

Scoring definitions:
Mission critical (+4)—This is the best case. Here, the disproportionate value discussed in Chapter 5 is clearly recognized by the customer as an organization.
Promising (0)—This is potential without perceived substance. In this situation, your value statement or proposition is of little interest to customer senior management, as it only relates indirectly to advancing their business direction.
Minimal (−3)—This means you have operational impact only. Your offering in this scenario produces no meaningful disproportionate value to the customer.
Unknown (−4)—You are unable to rank this criterion.

Coaching questions:
- What is the relationship between your offering and the customer's corporate initiatives?
- Can you articulate the customer's core business strategy?
- What is the relationship between the value impact you will have on the customer and your pricing?
- How does customer senior management perceive your company?
- Have you been able to create significant value for the customer in the past?
- Are you aligned with a Fox in the customer's organization?

4. Measurability: If you cannot measure it, it is not real. This is the one criterion that most contributes to the reality or soundness of value. Without an ability to measure the value that you actually provide or, at a minimum, to develop an indication of value, you risk:

- *Not getting credit for the success of your solution.* Value alone will not increase your currency within an account. That requires both value and recognition. If the right people do not see the good work that you do, you lose the opportunity to enhance key relationships through the recognition of performance.
- *Being forced into discounting.* Elasticity of demand, in terms of what people are willing to pay for something, is directly impacted by past

measurable performance. Three factors primarily drive this elasticity: price, value, and availability.

If you have in the past produced measured results and your competition has not, your competitive strength is increased and the price that you can command is higher, producing better margins.

- *The possibility of competitive displacement.* One of the best ways to penetrate a competitively held account is to introduce metrics that measure your competition's effectiveness in a particular area. Such assessment devices can be surgically precise in identifying improvement opportunities that translate into sales opportunities.

Scoring definitions:
Trackable (+3)—This is the best case. This suggests that the customer is ready, willing, and able to actively engage in results tracking:

- *Ready* indicates that the customer knows what to measure and how to measure it.
- *Willing* suggests that customer senior management is not opposed to the internal accountability that will result, which can sometimes be a cultural or philosophical issue.
- *Able* indicates that the necessary resources are in place to collect and analyze data.

Accessible (0)—This means your criteria are more soft than hard. In this case, the customer supports the measuring of results, but the soft or qualitative nature of the metrics makes the results somewhat interpretive. This can lead senior management or nonsupporters to discount your impact within the account.
Problematic (–3)—This means you have lack of measures. Identified measures or metrics either don't exist or are not practical to track. In some cases other variables beyond your control will influence the measures, diminishing their validity.
Unknown (–4)—You are unable to rank this criterion.

Coaching questions:
- How is value currently being tracked and measured on projects similar to this one?

- Is the customer seeking new and innovative approaches to understanding, measuring, and improving this part of his or her business?
- How does our measurement approach differ from that of our competitor?
- Will the customer's internal culture support tracking and measurement?
- Does the necessary interdepartmental cooperation within the customer's organization exist?
- Will any customer individuals receive a bonus based on the results achieved?

Again, the scoring for this Can we add value? phase, or metric, of the opportunity evaluator process is

- *Solid:* The value is real and significant to the customer. It is measurable with the necessary systems to support actual measurement in place or if not, the customer is willing to build them in a timely manner.
- *Emerging:* The value is significant to the customer, but measurability is questionable.
- *Weak:* Measurement in any quantitative fashion is not possible, but qualitative indicators of value may exist.
- *Nonexistent:* Tracking or measuring performance is simply not possible.

In this second phase of the process, illustrated in Table 8.2, you are dealing with the next seven criteria, which measure the quality of the business that you are pursuing. It represents the counterbalancing value that you will expect your organization to receive from the customer if you deliver on your value statement or proposition. Let's examine each of them:

5. Geography/resourceable: Account access can be everything. Have you ever been sitting next to a customer when a competitor calls him or her on the phone? If you have, you know the power of being local to an account, a situation in which you can formally and informally gain access to people and work face-to-face with them.

Table 8.2   **Major Opportunity Evaluator II: Should We Pursue? Metrics Chart**

Criteria	Scale		Your Scores
5. Geography/ Resourceable	+2: Local 0: Not an issue	−1: Coverage issues −2: Remote	
6. Time Frame	+3: Immediate 0: Reasonable	−3: Unreasonable −4: Unknown	
7. Funding	+3: Funds in place 0: Adequate	−3: No budget −4: Unknown	
8. Customer Competence	+3: Experienced 0: Supportive	−3: Inhibits −4: Unknown	
9. Risk Assessment	+3: Low 0: Manageable	−3: High −4: Unknown	
10. Profitability to Us	+4: Premium 0: Acceptable	−3: Unacceptable −4: Unknown	
11. Future value to Us	+4: Asset 0: Referenceable	−3: Unreferenceable −4: Unknown	

Scoring Key:
❏ +13 to +22: **Excellent**
❏ +3 to +12: **Good**
❏ −11 to +2: **Marginal**
❏ −26 to −12: **Undesirable**

Scoring definitions:
Local (+2)—This is the geographically ideal situation. With the account within driving distance, your ability to more rapidly build a strong support base creating good sales momentum with reduced cost of sales translates into increased sales effectiveness. In addition, it allows you to bring in sales support resources whenever needed, also with reduced cost.
Not an issue (0)—Logistics are manageable. Although not as close as a local account, the travel requirements do not present a problem in terms of costs, sales, or serviceability. Cost of sales and opportunity cost—that is, the time away from other accounts due to travel time—is acceptable. In some cases, this is due to your having other accounts in geographic proximity to the new opportunity.

Coverage issues (–1)—Account access is difficult. Sales and service travel will need to be carefully managed. Exposure to customer individuals will be limited, compromising sales effectiveness.

Remote (–2)—Account access is very difficult. Sales coverage is definitely an issue, decreasing sales effectiveness and possibly protracting the sales cycle. Overcoming this difficulty will require more travel time and expense, thereby increasing cost of sales and opportunity cost.

Coaching questions:
- Do you have other accounts in the same geographical area?
- Do you have any referral accounts in that area?
- Is your competition local or remote to the account?
- How competitive will the sales situation be?
- How support-intensive will this sale be?
- Would the customer be willing and able to travel to your location for certain meetings?

6. Time frame: Fast is best. Short sales cycles are great, not only due to your ability to generate the business quickly, but also because a short, fast-paced sales cycle is easier to manage from a competitive point of view. If you are in the lead, shortness of cycle is even more critical because time is not in your favor when there is only one way to go—down.

Scoring definitions:
Immediate (+3)—This is a very short sales cycle opportunity for your territory.
Reasonable (0)—This is an average sales cycle for your territory.
Unreasonable (–3)—This is a long sales cycle, again for your territory. These accounts are generally considered as early development stage accounts.
Unknown (–4)—You are unable to rank this criterion.

Coaching questions:
- Is there a driving mechanism for this opportunity?
- Does the customer have experience with this type of purchase, or will an educational process be required, thereby unavoidably lengthening the sales cycle?

- Is the budget approved, or will a funding cycle add time to the sales cycle?
- How accessible are the customer individuals who will have to approve the buy decision?
- How is the decision-making process structured?
- Is a Fox driving the acquisition?

7. Funding: This is a critical element to establishing a close condition. As you will recall from Chapter 2, a close condition does not exist until the customer is ready, willing, and able to make a commitment. Funding availability is, in turn, key to the able state.

♨ A Selling Fox, *whose eye is focused on the close, always monitors the funding process from the start.*

Scoring definitions:
Funds committed (+3)—You're good to go. Funds to support an acquisition are in place and the approval process is defined and manageable.
Adequate (0)—Funding is present. Here, the approval process necessary to release the funds is not clear.
No budget (–3)—Funding is not present. Funding is not available and it appears unlikely the funds can be successfully pulled from another project in the near term.
Unknown (–4)—You are unable to rank this criterion.

Coaching questions:
- What is the process for determining budget?
- Who has or had to approve the budget?
- Can funds be pulled from another project in the near term?
- Is it possible to move the acquisition from that of a capital budget expenditure to an expense item, such as would be the case with a lease purchase?
- What business factors are impacting budgets?
- Will the acquisition generate revenue or reduce costs, underscoring the need for a solid value proposition?

8. Customer competence: Your best success will be with a competent customer. Keep in mind that customers that are on the uphill side of the learning curve, relative to the implementation of your type of solution, will be:

- More susceptible to competitive influence.
- Less able to understand the significance of your product's or solution's capabilities.
- In a steep learning mode, requiring a strong educational process from a sales point of view. This translates into additional time and longer sales cycles.

Scoring definitions:

Experienced (+3)—This is the best case. In this situation, the customer is familiar with what is required to ensure success, as evidenced by the customer's participation in your building an engagement plan, as discussed in Chapter 2 (Table 2.2) to support the acquisition.

Supportive (0)—The customer has had a generally similar experience in the past or recognizes the need to hire people. In this scenario, the customer understands the importance of having competent people on the project, either through past experience or through training.

Inhibits (−3)—You have a problem. The worst-case situation is one in which the customer is not competent and does not know that he or she is not competent.

Unknown (−4)—You are unable to rank this criterion.

Coaching questions:

- Will the customer individuals who will be assigned to this project be fully dedicated to it, working on a full-time basis?
- If a key customer individual were to leave, how would you and the customer respond?
- Is there past evidence of success within the account, relative to this type of application?
- Is there a way to introduce this customer to other customers who have been very successful with similar sales solutions?
- Does the customer's operating philosophy support investing in training company employees?
- Does it make sense to recommend that the customer consider engaging certain consulting services to help ensure success?

9.   Risk assessment: Understanding the risk of failure, as it relates to the installation, is second nature to a Selling Fox. The two dimensions of risk are:

- What is the magnitude of the risk?
- How manageable is the risk?

Large amounts of risk can be assumed if it is manageable and if the potential payoff is acceptable. On the other hand, even small amounts of risk that are not manageable can be dangerous.

Scoring definitions:
Low (+3)—The fit between the customer's needs and your solution is excellent. History tells you that any downside to this installation is minimal.
Manageable (0)—The risks that exist can be identified and proactively managed. The balance of risk to reward is acceptable. Perhaps you will be doing some significant customization for the customer or the account requires a new application for your product. It may be your first installation of a new product that your company has just introduced. In any case, there is risk, but it is manageable.
High (–3)—This indicates unacceptable risk and poor manageability. This is a dangerous combination independent of the potential reward, as the downside is not limited to what takes place in the account that you are pursuing. It could also impact other accounts that might suffer for lack of attention and resources—opportunity cost.
Unknown (–4)—You are unable to rank this criterion.

Coaching questions:
- How do you *feel* about this sales situation?
- How do the risks involved compare to those in your past experiences?
- Would it be appropriate for the customer to take some ownership for the risk involved?
- Is your company prepared to deal with the risk in a timely manner?
- What effect could this have on your other accounts?
- What does the risk involved represent in financial terms?

10. Profitability to us: The counterbalance to risk is profit. Profitability is a function of the customer's perceived value at the business, political, and cultural levels. Not long ago in a New England town, a theater company was putting on a performance and wanted to thank the community for all the wonderful support that it had received. It elected not to charge admission. When the show opened, *virtually no one showed up!* The next year, another very good play opened, but this time the theater company charged admission, and the show was a sellout. Thinking that the problem the first year was one of becoming known for its productions, the company decided that for its third-year production, which would be their best ever, the company would go back to not charging. At opening, again virtually no one attended. For many, perception is reality (Selling Foxes know that *rarely* is perception reality). In this case, not charging for admission translated into a perception of no value. As we have discussed, other factors like price and the presence of competitive alternatives also affect what a customer will pay, but *managing* the customer's perception of value is core to winning profitable business.

Scoring definitions:
Premium (+4)—This indicates a high value perception. Here the customer recognizes the value that you can provide.

- From a business point of view—your value statement or proposition.
- From a political point of view—advancing the personal agendas of key people.
- From a cultural point of view—personifying their operating philosophy in how you work with them.
- From a relationship point of view—the customer takes into account your future potential value to himself or herself.

Acceptable (0)—This is not great, but okay. The value to you and to your company is acceptable, considering the amount of time and effort that you will put into the account and any nonmonetary value that the account represents, such as providing referrals in the future.
Unacceptable (–3)—This indicates undesirable business. In the absence of extenuating factors, this is not good business to pursue.
Unknown (–4)—You are unable to rank this criterion.

Coaching questions:
- Does the customer recognize the value that you can provide on a more holistic level—business, political, cultural, and relationship?
- Who within the account will shape the customer's perception of value?
- What is the relationship between that value and the appropriate Fox's personal agenda?
- Is your value statement or proposition tied to a customer corporate initiative in order to provide disproportionate value?
- Have you linked your value statement or proposition to something that the customer has already internalized or taken to heart, so to speak?
- Are you to some extent an extension of the customer's Power Base as it relates to what you do, and does your work with your customers reflect what they hold to be important, in terms of operating values?

11. Future value to us: Assess strategic value. In many accounts, a great company-to-company relationship begins with a very successful installation. When customer senior management then recognizes that success, it sets the stage for strategic value that may manifest itself as:

- Repeat orders
- Strong referrals to other companies/prospects
- An enhancement to your company's reputation and credibility, especially if the customer company is well regarded in its industry
- An opportunity to beta test new products
- A partnering or joint development opportunity between the two companies

Scoring definitions:
Asset (+4)—There is tangible value beyond the sale. In this case, the value that we discussed previously exists in a very real form in which you can essentially draw a line, directly or indirectly, from the sales situation to future sales.
Referenceable (0)—The company will serve as a good reference for you. It is not viewed as a bellwether company in its industry, but will be a nice addition to your referral list.

Unreferenceable (−3)—Value is unknown or the reference is unwilling. In most cases, an unreferenceable account is one that for all intents and purposes is small, unknown in the marketplace, or has a formal policy prohibiting the use of the company's name or disclosure of information. It may also be a company that has a reputation within its industry that you and your company do not want to be associated with at this time.

Unknown (−4)—You are unable to rank this criterion.

Coaching questions:
- How is the customer company viewed within its industry?
- Who specifically would provide referrals?
- What would motivate these individuals to provide strong referrals?
- Is there any partnering potential with the customer?
- Is there an opportunity to publish a joint article with the customer company relative to the work you will do with it?
- How will winning this order impact your competitors in the future?

As you can see, qualifying major opportunities is a thought process that builds a foundation for a sales campaign that will allow you to compete with confidence. Establishing that a balance exists between the value you will provide the customer and that which you will receive back will help ensure:

- Management support within your own company
- Minimum negative impact on other active sales situations and accounts
- That you avoid "black hole" accounts, which are a drain on your company's resources, never providing you with profitable business in return
- That you develop maximum strategic value from accounts

Using the major opportunity evaluator gives you the ability to determine quickly and objectively whether the value that you believe you can provide to the customer is solid, emerging, weak, or nonexistent in comparison to the value that you expect to receive, identifying it as excellent, good, marginal, or undesirable business.

Assessing Your Competitive Position

Now, let's transition to the competitive side of the equation, first look-ing at how well you are aligned with the customer in terms of your pro-posed solution, history working together, and philosophical or cultural compatibility. Table 8.3 can assist you in organizing this information.

Unlike what we have done so far, we will be looking at these three criteria from both your point of view and that of your primary competi-tor in order to determine whether you have a dominant, at parity, or dis-advantaged competitive position. Again, let's review the criteria one at a time:

Table 8.3 **Major Opportunity Evaluator III: Can We Compete? Metrics Chart**

Criteria	Scale		Your Scores
12. Solution Compatibility	+4: Strong 0: Adequate	−3: Weak −4: Unknown	
Competitor's Solution Compatibility	+4: Weak 0: Adequate	−3: Strong −4: Unknown	
13. Customer History	+4: An asset 0: Neutral	−3: A liability −4: Unknown	
Competitor's Customer History	+4: A liability 0: Neutral	−3: An asset −4: Unknown	
14. Philosophical Alignment	+4: Culturally aligned 0: Manageable	−3: Significant problems −4: Unknown	
Competitor's Philosophical Alignment	+4: Significant problems 0: Manageable	−3: Culturally aligned −4: Unknown	

Scoring Key:
❒ +12 to +24: **Dominant**
❒   −9 to +11: **At Parity**
❒ −24 to −10: **Disadvantaged**

12. Solution compatibility: Meeting the customer's needs. This is an issue of fit, but recognize that as objective as any decision-making process or matrix may appear, it is still very subjective. Both the weighting of criteria and how well a company actually complies with them is often a matter of judgment. Once again, we find ourselves dealing with perceptions and politics.

Scoring definitions:
Strong (+4)—This indicates excellent fit. Here, your solution addresses all of the customer's buying criteria in a robust manner.
Adequate (0)—This is an acceptable approach to meeting the customer's most significant needs. In this case, your solution will do the job, but does not address all of the customer's buying criteria.
Weak (–3)—This indicates poor fit. Unlike determining that a sales opportunity represents bad business, this is not a go-or-no-go criterion. You may not be able to address all of the customer's needs at a given point in time; however, you may be able to in the future if new product capabilities are in the works. In that event, a *migration path strategy*—addressing a subset of the customer's needs in the short term and the balance over time—could be just the ticket.
Unknown (–4)—You are unable to rank this criterion.

Coaching questions:
- Which customer individuals were responsible for the construction of the decision-making criteria?
- Are any of these people aligned with the competition?
- Are they in the Power Base?
- Are you aligned with the appropriate Fox?
- How have you been innovative in addressing the customer's needs?
- Have you influenced the decision-making criteria? If so, how?

Competitor's solution compatibility: How well does your primary competitor meet the customer's needs? Rate this competitive criterion, putting yourself in the competition's shoes—be objective.

Competitive scoring:
Weak (+4)—This indicates poor competitive fit with the customer's needs.
Adequate (0)—This is an acceptable approach to meeting the customer's most significant needs.

Strong (–3)—This indicates excellent fit. Such a rating underscores the need to consider an indirect sales strategy, as the quality of the competitor company's solution will probably move it to implement a direct strategy.

Unknown (–4)—You are unable to rank this criterion.

13. Customer history: Being a known entity. Some people believe that your history with a particular customer becomes an asset if everything has gone well. That is true, but even better is when you have had problems with a customer and have succeeded in solving them, ultimately exceeding the customer's expectations. Everyone looks good when all has gone well, but when problems surface, how you handle them can make all the difference. The key, when confronted with this type of adversity, is to:

- Accept ownership for the problem, whatever it is.
- Focus on solving the problem quickly.
- Then address the secondary problems that were created.
- Keep the customer actively involved.
- Make certain that when all is resolved, the customer receives more value than would have been received if the original problem had not come about.
- Make certain that the appropriate Foxes within the customer organization are aware of how well you handled the problem.

No one likes problems, but they can often provide the fastest road to building a trust-based relationship with a Fox.

Scoring definitions:
An asset (+4)—You are viewed as a strategic resource. In this situation, you and your company are a known entity, with a strong support base within the account.

Neutral (0)—You have minimal history. In some cases, you will have worked with the customers, but because your involvement with them has not been high enough profile, perhaps aggravated by frequent changes in sales coverage, you are really not well known to them.

A liability (–3)—You have bad history. This is a real problem not only in this account, but also in the marketplace. If ever you find this situation in your territory, take steps to evaluate the problem and address it immediately.

Unknown (–4)—You are unable to rank this criterion.

Coaching questions:
- How have problems in the account been handled in the past?
- Did your company quickly accept responsibility for any problems?
- Have changes in sales coverage impacted the customer relationship? If so, how?
- What is the customer's view of the value your company has provided to them?
- How much personal currency do you have in the account?
- Have executive-to-executive relationships been established and maintained between the companies?

Competitor's customer history: What does the past say about your primary competitor's relationship with the account? Rate this competitive criterion, again putting yourself in the competition's shoes, endeavoring to be very objective.

Competitive scoring:
A liability (+4)—Bridges have been burnt.
Neutral (0)—They have little to no history.
An asset (–3)—A strong support base exists. This is a real problem. To succeed will probably require a shift in the political structure of the account. Go back to the tools presented in Chapter 7 on de-installing a competitor in a major account to evaluate whether the business is worth pursuing.
Unknown (–4)—You are unable to rank this criterion.

14. **Philosophical alignment:** Seeing eye to eye. Before two companies can come together on an important project, a philosophical and political merger must take place. Success requires that the appropriate people on both sides share certain values that will shape their views as to how implementation will actually take place. Examples of this can be seen in how people view:

- The need to communicate with others
- A bias for action, regarding expediency as very important
- Teamwork and delegation
- The discipline of planning and the need for process

Perhaps most important in this intangible, but very important area is the understanding of two key principles.

Ⲙ *Foxes personify the operating philosophy of their organizations, as they are instrumental in shaping it through their Power Base.*

A Selling Fox knows this and realizes that to maximize compatibility with a customer Fox, to align your mutual interests he or she must also appropriately personify that same operating philosophy.

Ⲙ *Foxes believe that how an achievement is realized is often as important as the achievement itself.*

To know how people will proceed in terms of what they hold to be important operationally is to know how they will react in the future—to problems, to new opportunities, and in the absence of management supervision or oversight. If a Fox is aware of a particular situation, he or she is generally able to predict how people will respond based upon his or her understanding as to what they believe in operationally. A well-defined work ethic is a strong predictor of future performance.

Scoring definitions:
Culturally aligned (+4)—You share common values. In this best-case scenario, you understand the operating philosophies of both organizations, what they have in common in terms of overlap, and where they are different. The point is this: they do not need to be the same; they only need to be *compatible*, with manageable differences. Generally, this condition exists when a Fox is involved on each side of the equation, creating a high degree of manageability.
Manageable (0)—Reasonable compatibility exists. Here, philosophical issues will not be a problem if the project time frame is not too long and if no major problem arises.

Significant problems (–3)—Opposing values spell disaster. Other than a hands-off, plug-and-play, commodity-type sales offering that requires no organizational overlap of the supplier and customer, this situation will breed adversity very quickly. Any accomplishments realized on either side will most likely be discounted by the other. It is a relationship state created by contrasting values. Although these values are intangible to most of the world, the resulting conflict will be very real and tangible. As a Selling Fox, never discount the intangible.

Unknown (–4)—You are unable to rank this criterion.

Coaching questions:
- What values does your organization hold to be important?
- Who is the "keeper" of these values?
- What values does the customer hold to be important?
- Who is the "keeper" of those values?
- Do the customer's values support or conflict with those of your organization?
- Are both companies' "value keepers" involved in the project?

Competitor's philosophical alignment: Does your primary competitor personify the customer's work ethic? Is your competitor a Selling Fox? You may want to approach this issue by focusing on the people you feel the primary competitor is most likely calling on in the account. Get to know them and what they believe in relative to their operating philosophies.

Competitive scoring:
Significant problems (+4)—They have significant incompatibility.
Manageable (0)—They have reasonable compatibility.
Culturally aligned (–3)—They share common values. In this case, the competition is probably very well aligned with a Fox, who more than anyone else in an organization can teach or familiarize suppliers regarding his or her company's operating philosophy and its significance.
Unknown (–4)—You are unable to rank this criterion.

As you add up your scores for the Can we compete? metric of the major opportunity evaluator, you will understand more clearly whether you have a dominant, at parity, or disadvantaged competitive position. You will also develop insight into any historical or philosophical alignment problems that might exist, as well as improve your ability to assess your primary competitor. For many salespeople, this is quite difficult. If alignment problems do exist, you can be confident that they will diminish your competitive strength over time.

The last segment of this four-phase process centers on the degree to which you are aligned to win. Unlike the Can we compete? metric, which is somewhat out of your control, *how* you sell will determine your score for the four specific criteria in the Are we aligned to win? metric shown in Table 8.4. Again, score yourself and your primary competitor.

15. Decision-making process leverage: Managing the decision-making process to generate maximum competitive advantage. The components to this effort consist of

- Understanding just who within the customer's organization will play what role(s) in the decision-making process
- Determining who is in the Power Base
- Developing insight into key individuals' personal agendas
- Assessing who might influence the people responsible for the decision-making process
- Understanding the decision-making criteria and how those criteria might be influenced.

Scoring definitions:
Strong (+4)—The deal is wired, so to speak. This is most often the case in a creating demand type of account, in which you have been instrumental in shaping the opportunity and therefore the decision-making criteria.
Adequate (0)—You have little leverage. This is where most salespeople start when they are new to an account; however, before the halfway point is reached in the sales cycle, the salesperson should be much stronger, with a score of at least +2.
Weak (–3)—You have a complete lack of information and leverage.
Unknown (–4)—You are unable to rank this criterion.

Table 8.4 **Major Opportunity Evaluator IV: Are We Aligned to Win? Metrics Chart**

Criteria	Scale		Your Scores
15. Decision-Making Process Leverage	+4: Strong 0: Adequate	−3: Weak −4: Unknown	
Competitor's Decision Leverage	+4: Weak 0: Adequate	−3: Strong −4: Unknown	
16. Political Leverage	+4: Agendas "hooked" 0: Limited relationships	−3: Disconnected −4: Unknown	
Competitor's Political Leverage	+4: Disconnected 0: Limited relationships	−3: Agendas "hooked" −4: Unknown	
17. Executive Sponsorship	+4: Strong 0: Emerging	−3: Weak −4: Unknown	
Competitor's Executive Sponsorship	+4: Weak 0: Emerging	−3: Strong −4: Unknown	
18. Established Momentum	+4: Strong 0: Gaining	−3: Losing −4: Unknown	
Competitor's Established Momentum	+4: Losing 0: Gaining	−3: Strong −4: Unknown	

Scoring Key:
- ❑ +24 to +32: **Strong**
- ❑ +13 to +23: **Growing**
- ❑ −9 to +12: **Tentative**
- ❑ −32 to −10: **Disconnected**

Coaching questions:
- Can you map out the formal decision-making process?
- Who might influence the process informally, and why?
- Who within the customer's organization constructed the decision-making matrix that scores suppliers against customer requirements?
- Is a committee involved?
- Who has to approve the decision and how is the approval process structured?
- How does what you know about the account compare with decisions that have been made in the past?

Competitor's decision leverage: Is the decision-making criteria aligned with the competition's strengths?

Competitive scoring:
Weak (+4)—They have no competitive leverage.
Adequate (0)—They have little leverage.
Strong (–3)—The buying criteria is designed around the competition's strengths. You need to understand how this came about. If the competition is wired, then its support base is probably a lot more extensive than you have recognized.
Unknown (–4)—You are unable to rank this criterion.

16. **Political leverage:** Tapping the power within an account. Influence drives sales and there is no more significant influence than that which exists within the customer's own political structure. To tap this power, Selling Foxes will:

- Map out the Power Base and identify the influential people within an organization.
- Identify the appropriate Fox.
- Determine whether any form of customer internal political competition exists—that is, power struggles, which reflect competing personal agendas, or power plays, which are similar, but are detrimental to the customer's company.
- Align with the more powerful side of the power struggle or, in the case of a power play, avoid both sides, as this type of political activ-

ity is parasitic to a company. Power plays exist when powerful individuals within an organization are working to advance their personal agendas at the expense of their company.

- Align with the appropriate Fox by understanding his or her personal agenda, positioning yourself as a resource to advance that agenda, and personifying the Fox's work ethic or operating philosophy.

Scoring definitions:
Agendas aligned (+4)—You have solid alignment with the right Fox. In this situation, you will be able to significantly influence the decision-making process.
Limited relationships (0)—You have no power on tap. At this point, you have not yet tapped into the Power Base to increase your competitive strength.
Disconnected (–3)—You have the wrong alignment. Here, you are working with people who are in opposition to the Power Base, perhaps on the wrong side of a power struggle.
Unknown (–4)—You are unable to rank this criterion.

Coaching questions:
- Who is in the Power Base? (Use the Fox Evaluator tool, Table 5.1, to help you determine this.)
- Who is the appropriate Fox with whom to align, and why? Again, consider using the Fox Evaluator to help in making this determination.
- Is a power struggle active? If so, what are the issues and how do they relate to the sales situation?
- Who will most probably win the power struggle?
- Is a power play active, and can it be avoided?
- What is the Fox's personal agenda and how can you align yourself so that you are positioned as a resource to advancing that agenda?

Competitor's political leverage: Has the competition aligned with the right Fox?

Competitive scoring:
Disconnected (+4)—They have the wrong alignment.
Limited relationships (0)—They have not tapped the political strength of the customer organization.

Agendas aligned (–3)—They have solid alignment with the right Fox. In this situation, look for any power struggles that might exist, along with the opportunity to align with a Fox who is politically opposed to the Fox who supports your competition. Also, make it a point to understand that Fox's personal agenda even though he or she is aligned with the competition.
Unknown (–4)—You are unable to rank this criterion.

17. Executive sponsorship: Building supporters and allies within the customer's executive ranks. This is largely a function of understanding and establishing the potential to advance the business direction of certain customer departments as they relate to your business while advancing the personal agendas of the executives responsible for those departments. To be successful in this aspect of competitive selling requires that you establish executive credibility early on with a new customer, which will in turn be dependent on your level of personal currency as is discussed in Chapter 5.

Scoring definitions:
Strong (+4)—Key customer executives perceive a degree of dependency on you, evidenced by their support and confidence in you.
Emerging (0)—You are on the right path. Here, you have no doubt begun to establish credibility at the executive levels. The potential to advance the customer's business is recognized, suggesting that it is time for you to set specific objectives for how you will move your score on this criterion into the Strong category.
Weak (–3)—Your value positioning is not established. Calling high, as discussed in Chapter 5, should be your highest priority if it makes sense to pursue this opportunity.
Unknown (–4)—You are unable to rank this criterion.

Coaching questions:
- What is your Currency Tabulator score for this account? Refer to Table 5.3, the Currency Tabulator.
- Where are you in the calling high process, as discussed in Chapter 5?
- Is your value positioning or value statement linked to a customer corporate initiative?

- Can you identify all of the customer executives that are a part of or that could influence the decision-making and approval processes?
- Of those executives, who is in the Power Base (See Table 5.1)?
- Who are the Foxes and what are their personal agendas?

Competitor's executive sponsorship: How well is the competition aligned with customer senior management?

Competitive scoring:
Weak (+4)—Competition has a distinct lack of executive sponsorship.
Emerging (0)—If the competition leverages its contacts in order to align with a customer Fox, it will quickly move to a Strong status.
Strong (−3)—Competition is firmly aligned with customer executive manage-
ment. In this case, you should accelerate your efforts to get to the right Fox—look for power struggles within the account and capitalize on them.
Unknown (−4)—You are unable to rank this criterion.

18. Established momentum: Creating a dynamic. Momentum is all about networking with people in the account, selling to each person even if he or she is not part of the decision-making or approval processes. In fact, building momentum requires that you spend time with customer managers outside the purview of the sales situation, contacting:

- Users and people who will support the product
- Marketing, if your solution will impact the customer's positioning in its marketplace
- Sales, if you will enable the customer to become more competitive
- Finance, if you will have a financial impact on their business as articulated in your value proposition.

In short, get to all the appropriate people who orbit your solution. They will then begin to speak to each other, which will create the dynamic that produces momentum.

Scoring definitions:
Strong (+4)—You appear to be everywhere within the account. People are talking about your solution, almost creating a bit of a buzz, so to speak. You are in the zone, where everything feels right.

Gaining (0)—You have begun to tap people's agendas. You're moving in the right direction, but momentum has not yet ignited.

Losing (−3)—You are losing ground. Often, this is due to the negative disposition of a Fox who is using his or her influence to dissuade others from considering your solution.

Unknown (−4)—You are unable to rank this criterion.

Coaching questions:
- Are certain customer individuals setting up meetings for you with others in the account?
- How many people are in your support base?
- How many people are in the competition's support base?
- Are you aligned with a Fox, as to do so is to align with his or her Power Base, which boosts your momentum in an account?
- Customer groups accelerate momentum. Does a committee or other group, perhaps a task force, exist?
- Has the customer requested the use of your presentation or sales support materials, an indication of so-called inside selling, which produces another boost to momentum?

Competitor's established momentum: Has the competition created a groundswell within the account? Effective networking, with the customer's Power Base at the center of the effort, is very difficult to counter.

Competitive scoring:
Losing (+4)—You have them on the run.

Gaining (0)—The competition is moving in the right direction. Time, in this case, is not in your favor. Do everything possible to collapse the time frame of the sales cycle.

Strong (−3)—The competition is cooking. You need to do two things.

- Contain the sales situation if at all possible. If a driving mechanism is present, this will be difficult, but should still be attempted as long as it does not adversely affect the customer.
- Map out with whom the competition is networking and begin to

shadow them by making new contacts to better understand how the competition has created appeal with the customer. This will not be easy, but needs to be attempted in order to set direction to your ability to build stronger momentum.

Unknown (−4)—You are unable to rank this criterion.

Major Opportunity Evaluator Summary

We have now completed the structural review of the four phases to evaluating a major opportunity, along with discussing and illustrating the necessary metrics to determine quickly and objectively whether it should be pursued and can be won, from a competitive point of view. The Major Opportunity Evaluator sales tool, shown in Tables 8.5 and 8.6, walks you through a thought process that will become the foundation of your competitive sales campaign, enabling you to do a better job of strategic formulation and tactical planning. It also provides significant insight into the business value and competitive strength aspects of waging a competitive sales campaign, thus becoming one of the most powerful sales tools in the arsenal of a Selling Fox.

Interpreting the Results

The following guidelines will assist you in interpreting the results of applying the Major Opportunity Evaluator:

1. Always strive to uncover or develop excellent business, using the Should we pursue? metric.
What is our value estimation
of this opportunity?
Scoring key:
❑ +13 to +22: Excellent
❑　+3 to +12: Good
❑ −11 to　+2: Marginal
❑ −26 to −12: Undesirable

Table 8.5 **Major Opportunity Evaluator Results I & II: Business Value**

Can We Add Value?	Scale		Your Scores
1. Customer Involvement in Value Discovery	+3: Proactive 0: Receptive	−3: Passive −4: Unknown	
2. Driving Mechanism	+4: Clear/Urgent 0: Clear	−3: Unclear −4: Unknown	
3. Business Impact	+4: Mission critical 0: Promising	−3: Minimal −4: Unknown	
4. Measurability	+3: Trackable 0: Accessible	−3: Problematic −4: Unknown	

Should We Pursue?	Scale		Your Scores
5. Geography/ Resourceable	+2: Local 0: Not an issue	−1: Coverage issues −2: Remote	
6. Time Frame	+3: Immediate 0: Reasonable	−3: Unreasonable −4: Unknown	
7. Funding	+3: Funds in place 0: Adequate	−3: No budget −4: Unknown	
8. Customer Competence	+3: Experienced 0: Supportive	−3: Inhibits −4: Unknown	
9. Risk Assessment	+3: Low 0: Manageable	−3: High −4: Unknown	
10. Profitability to Us	+4: Premium 0: Acceptable	−3: Unacceptable −4: Unknown	
11. Future value to Us	+4: Asset 0: Referenceable	−3: Unreferenceable −4: Unknown	

Table 8.6 **Major Opportunity Evaluator Results III & IV: Competitive Strength**

Can We Compete?	Scale		Your Scores
12. Solution Compatibility	+4: Strong 0: Adequate	−3: Weak −4: Unknown	
Competitor's Solution Compatibility	+4: Weak 0: Adequate	−3: Strong −4: Unknown	
13. Customer History	+4: An asset 0: Neutral	−3: A liability −4: Unknown	
Competitor's Customer History	+4: A liability 0: Neutral	−3: An asset −4: Unknown	
14. Philosophical Alignment	+4: Culturally aligned 0: Manageable	−3: Significant problems −4: Unknown	
Competitor's Philosophical Alignment	+4: Significant "disconnects" 0: Manageable	−3: Culturally aligned −4: Unknown	
15. Decision-Making Process Leverage	+4: Strong 0: Adequate	−3: Weak −4: Unknown	
Competitor's Decision Leverage	+4: Weak 0: Adequate	−3: Strong −4: Unknown	
16. Political Leverage	+4: Agendas aligned 0: Limited relationships	−3: Disconnected −4: Unknown	
Competitor's Political Leverage	+4: Disconnected 0: Limited relationships	−3: Agendas aligned −4: Unknown	

Are We Aligned to Win?	Scale		Your Scores
17. Executive Sponsorship	+4: Strong 0: Emerging	−3: Weak −4: Unknown	
Competitor's Executive Sponsorship	+4: Weak 0: Emerging	−3: Strong −4: Unknown	
18. Established Momentum	+4: Strong 0: Gaining	−3: Losing −4: Unknown	
Competitor's Established Momentum	+4: Losing 0: Gaining	−3: Strong −4: Unknown	

2. Be certain that the Should we pursue? and Can we add value? scores are appropriately balanced.

What is our value estimation of this opportunity?

Scoring key:

- ❏ +13 to +22: Excellent
- ❏ +3 to +12: Good
- ❏ –11 to +2: Marginal
- ❏ –26 to –12: Undesirable

What is our competitive position in adding customer value?

Scoring key:

- ❏ +7 to +14: Solid
- ❏ –1 to +6: Emerging
- ❏ –8 to –2: Weak

3. Set specific sales objectives to improve your Can we compete? and Are we aligned to win? scores—reassess your progress frequently.

What is our position in relation to our primary competitor?

Scoring key:

- ❏ +12 to +24: Dominant
- ❏ –9 to +11: At parity
- ❏ –24 to –10: Disadvantaged

To what degree are we aligned to win?

Scoring key:

- ❏ +24 to +32: Strong
- ❏ +13 to +23: Growing
- ❏ –9 to +12: Tentative
- ❏ –32 to –10: Disconnected

4. Monitor your overall competitive position and sales forecast, determining whether the business is

- Secure—you are confident of a win.
- At risk—the business could go either way (50-50).
- Severely at risk—you feel that you are losing.

This is based upon the combined scores of Can we compete? and Are we aligned? metrics.

Sales forecast scoring key:

- ❏ +36 to +56: Secure
- ❏ +4 to +35: At risk
- ❏ –56 to +3: Severely at risk

5. Prioritize your sales focus using Table 8.7 and the scores from the Should we pursue? and Are we aligned to win? metrics to create the fastest road to quota.

Table 8.7 **Prioritizing Opportunities**

What Is Our Value Estimation of This Opportunity?	Can We Compete? and Are We Aligned?	
1. Excellent	Severely at risk	Highest priority
2. Excellent	At risk	·
3. Good	Severely at risk	·
4. Excellent	Secure	·
5. Good	At risk	·
6. Good	Secure	·
7. Marginal	Secure	·
8. Marginal	At risk	·
9. Marginal	Severely at risk	Lowest priority

As you develop your territory and all the sales opportunities that characterize it, this prioritization will help keep you focused on opportunities that most rapidly advance you to quota.

Short Cycle Opportunity Evaluator

Pursuing short cycle, transaction-driven business requires a different approach to qualifying opportunities. There simply is not enough time to initiate an 18-point evaluation criterion, nor is it necessary. If a sales situation is highly competitive or you sense that you are losing, you can always use the Major Opportunity Evaluator to drive a more thorough thought process, leaving no stone unturned. But for most short sales cycle opportunities, the following eight-point Opportunity Evaluation sales tool shown in Table 8.8, which also measures your competitor's position and leverage in the account, is recommended.

Setting Strategy

As you work with this sales tool, you will discover that criteria numbers 1, 5, 6, 7, and 8 are central to the establishment of the right sales strategy (direct, indirect, divisional, or containment). A Selling Fox knows that even fast-paced, somewhat commodity-oriented selling requires strategy and analysis, if you are to consistently enjoy high sales hit rates. The thinking behind this correlation is the following:

- *Driving mechanism* determines whether a containment strategy is possible.
- *Product or solution compatibility* is an important component to establishing the superiority necessary to implement a direct sales strategy, from a product point of view. It will also provide insight into the appropriateness of going divisional, in which you partition off a part of the application, complementing the competitor's solution.
- *Decision-making process leverage* is critical to the planning and execution of an indirect strategy in which you plan to change the ground rules and alter the decision-making criteria. It is also important to going direct.
- *Political leverage and executive sponsorship* are criteria that characterize your support base within an account, clearly indicating whether you have sufficient competitive strength to go direct or indirect to defeat the competition.

Short Cycle—Should We Pursue?

Criteria numbers 2, 3, 4, and 5 make up the Short cycle—should we pursue? phase of the opportunity evaluation process, suggesting whether the business is excellent, good, marginal, or bad. Because of the divergent nature of short-cycle selling, it is recommended that you modify the provided scoring ranges to reflect the products, services, and territory that you are dealing with in your day-to-day selling activities.

Like the sales tool calibration process, run the short cycle opportunity evaluator shown in Table 8.9 against sales opportunities that you know represent excellent business and, at the other end of the spectrum, undesirable business you elected not to pursue. That will provide the range for scoring particular to your territory.

Short Cycle—Can We Win?

A slightly different expression of what we discussed in the major opportunity arena, this important competitive determination is based upon

Table 8.8 **Short Cycle Opportunity Evaluator I Chart**

Criteria	Scale		Your Scores
1. Driving Mechanism	+4: Clear/urgent 0: Clear	−3: Unclear −4: Unknown	
2. Geography/ Resourceable	+2: Local 0: Not an issue	−1: Coverage issues −2: Remote	
3. Time Frame	+3: Immediate 0: Reasonable	−3: Unreasonable −4: Unknown	
4. Funding	+3: Funds in place 0: Adequate	−3: No budget −4: Unknown	
5. Solution Compatibility	+4: Strong 0: Adequate	−3: Weak −4: Unknown	
Competitor's Solution Compatibility	+4: Weak 0: Adequate	−3: Strong −4: Unknown	
6. Decision-Making Process Leverage	+4: Strong 0: Adequate	−3: Weak −4: Unknown	
Competitor's Decision Leverage	+4: Weak 0: Adequate	−3: Strong −4: Unknown	
7. Political Leverage	+4: Agendas "hooked" 0: Limited relationships	−3: Disconnected −4: Unknown	
Competitor's Political Leverage	+4: Disconnected 0: Limited relationships	−3: Agendas "hooked" −4: Unknown	
8. Executive Sponsorship	+4: Strong 0: Emerging	−3: Weak −4: Unknown	
Competitor's Executive Sponsorship	+4: Weak 0: Emerging	−3: Strong −4: Unknown	

Table 8.9　**Short Cycle Opportunity Evaluator II: Should We Pursue? Metrics Chart**

Criteria	Scale		Your Scores
2. Geography/ Resourcable	+2: Local 0: Not an issue	−1: Coverage issues −2: Remote	
3. Time Frame	+3: Immediate 0: Reasonable	−3: Unreasonable −4: Unknown	
4. Funding	+3: Funds in place 0: Adequate	−3: No budget −4: Unknown	
5. Product or Solution Compatibility	+4: Strong 0: Adequate	−3: Weak −4: Unknown	

Scoring Key:
❐　+8 to +12: **Excellent**
❐　 0 to +7: **Good**
❐　−6 to −1: **Marginal**
❐　−14 to −7: **Bad**

criteria numbers 5, 6, 7, and 8, shown in Table 8.10. Again, rank both yourself and your primary competitor. As in the Should we pursue? metric, it is recommended that you modify the provided scoring ranges to reflect the specific nature of your territory and the types of competitors that you deal with on a day-to-day basis. Monitor your overall competitive position and sales forecast, as you did with the major opportunity evaluator, determining whether the business is

- Secure—you are confident of a win.
- At risk—the business could go either way (50-50).
- Severely at risk—you feel that you are losing.

Whether you are moving fast, with large numbers of active short cycle sales situations, or carefully assessing the merits of launching into a lengthy sales campaign to win a new major account, the opportunity evaluation process and the opportunity evaluator sales tools are the way of the Selling Fox. They will serve you well as a measurable way to im-

Table 8.10   **Short Cycle Opportunity Evaluator III: Can We Win? Metrics Chart**

Criteria	Scale		Your Scores
5. Solution Compatibility	+4: Strong 0: Adequate	–3: Weak –4: Unknown	
Competitor's Solution Compatibility	+4: Weak 0: Adequate	–3: Strong –4: Unknown	
6. Decision-Making Process Leverage	+4: Strong 0: Adequate	–3: Weak –4: Unknown	
Competitor's Decision Leverage	+4: Weak 0: Adequate	–3: Strong –4: Unknown	
7. Political Leverage	+4: Agendas "hooked" 0: Limited relationships	–3: Disconnected –4: Unknown	
Competitor's Political Leverage	+4: Disconnected 0: Limited relationships	–3: Agendas "hooked" –4: Unknown	
8. Executive Sponsorship	+4: Strong 0: Emerging	–3: Weak –4: Unknown	
Competitor's Executive Sponsorship	+4: Weak 0: Emerging	–3: Strong –4: Unknown	

Scoring Key:

❐ +21 to +32: **Secure**

❐ +2 to +20: **At Risk**

❐ –32 to +1: **Severely At Risk**

prove your hit rate and avert costly losses, while building a solid foundation to your territory and account development efforts.

The Fox Ethos

Adding to our list of Fox-like attributes as they relate to this chapter, we continue:

The Fox Ethos

Foxes like balance; Selling Foxes always evaluate risk (magnitude and manageability) versus reward.

Foxes are strategic; Selling Foxes know that even fast-paced, somewhat commodity-oriented selling requires strategy and analysis.

Foxes value time; Selling Foxes prioritize opportunities to optimize time and resources.

9

Are You a Selling Fox?

Are *you* a Selling Fox? How can you tell whether you are? Chapter 4 introduced the concept of self-assessment as it relates to your personal sales performance. The intent is to build a closed-loop feedback system to enhance your sales performance and to assure your success as a Selling Fox by:

- Assisting you in measuring your current levels of competitive selling ability
- Creating a self-development plan that defines your developmental goals, strategy, and tactics

This type of introspective objectivity is characteristic of both the rising and the established Selling Fox, constantly contributing to increased personal performance.

Expanding Your Self-Performance Rating

You will recall that in Chapter 4, we applied this self-development process to a number of critical sales techniques identified in Table 4.2, the Self-Performance Rating, assigning each a ranking of manageable (M), difficult (D), or hard (H). That initial evaluation process resulted in the formation of a highly relevant self-development plan, an example of which we discussed in Chapter 4, Sales Example 12—Self-Performance Rating.

Now that we have addressed additional selling techniques in the ensuing chapters, we can expand on the self-performance rating and development process to include:

- Calling high
- Implementing the indirect sales strategy
- Qualifying opportunities

We'll do a quick review of specifics for each of these technique areas, followed by an opportunity for you to rank your own performance in each competitive selling technique area according to the manageable, difficult, and hard rating scale. Again, it is this type of honest introspection that is characteristic of a Selling Fox.

Calling High

Let's break this important area of competitive selling down, looking at the key aspects to establishing and maintaining executive relationships. First, we review calling high.

Personifying the Fox ethos: This centers on the three core characteristics or attributes that help identify you as a Selling Fox:

- Not egocentric
- Good listener
- Mission driven

The more Fox-like you are, the more initiative customer Foxes will take to bond with you.

Fox hunting ability: This depends on effectively using the Fox Evaluator.

Hooking a customer executive's personal agenda: This means quickly building an understanding of a key person's political or organizational aspirations and positioning yourself as a resource to advance those aspirations.

Generating value statements: This means building high-impact, customer-specific qualitative expressions of value.

Generating value propositions: This means building high-impact, customer-specific quantitative expressions of value.

Identifying customer supporters and allies: This depends on effectively using the Contact Evaluator.

Assessing your executive credibility from a value point of view: This depends on effectively using the Currency Tabulator.

Implementing the seven-step executive calling process: This requires an ability to effectively execute each phase of the Calling High process that you will recall from Chapter 5:

1. Preparing for contact
2. Executive preconditioning
3. Making contact
4. The initial executive meeting
5. Defining your support base objectives
6. Developing your value proposition
7. The value acknowledgment executive meeting

Mastering the Indirect Sales Strategy

As you will recall from Chapter 6, the indirect strategy is the approach of choice for a Selling Fox due to its extreme effectiveness in highly competitive sales situations. From a self-development point of view, it is appropriate to look at two aspects of increasing your ability to build and deploy the indirect strategy:

Formulating indirect strategy: This requires effectively using the Indirect Strategy Matrix (Table 6.1), which identifies the critical components to a specific indirect strategy.

Performing a business analysis to assess the territorial cost of a competitive campaign: This requires effectively building an Account Terrain Map and a Territorial Business Impact Map (Tables 7.1 and 7.2).

Qualifying Opportunities

Determining where to focus your sales efforts while building a foundation of understanding to support a competitive sales campaign is essential to making and exceeding quota on a consistent basis. The qualifying process should be repeated throughout a sales cycle to continually keep you grounded. As you will recall from Chapter 8, the process differs, depending on whether you are considering the pursuit of a major opportunity or a short-cycle, more transaction-oriented deal.

Qualifying a major opportunity: This means effectively utilizing the 18-point criteria Major Opportunity Evaluation sales tool to determine:

- Can we add value?
- Should we pursue?
- Can we compete?
- Are we aligned to win?

Qualifying a short-cycle opportunity: This means effectively utilizing the eight-point criteria Short Cycle Opportunity Evaluation sales tool to determine:

- Should we pursue?
- Can we win?

We have now covered the key competitive selling techniques that a Selling Fox masters in order to effectively engage and defeat competition. Incorporating these new sales techniques into the earlier self-performance rating chart (Table 4.2) gives you an ability to determine quickly and accurately where your self-development focus needs to be concentrated in order to optimize your sales performance and continue your development as a Selling Fox. Table 9.1 is provided to assist you in rating your skills. You will recall that the rating designations for the chart are:

- M = Manageable
- D = Difficult
- H = Hard

When you have completed this comprehensive self-assessment, look at those techniques that present problems or developmental opportunities for you, and create a self-development plan that defines your developmental goals, strategy, and tactics. (*Note:* For a review on how to analyze the self-performance rating results and create a self-development plan, see Chapter 4.)

Table 9.1 **Expanded Self-Performance Rating Chart**

Selling Techniques	M	D	H	Comments
Asking directly for an order				
Probing for objections				
Jumping objections				
Blocking the competition				
Trapping to negative selling				
Trapping to price discounting				
Trapping to product deficiencies				
Preparing for loss recovery				
Personifying the Fox ethos				
Fox hunting				
Hooking a customer individual's personal agenda				
Generating Value Statements				
Generating Value Propositions				
Using the Contact Evaluator				
Using the Currency Tabulator				
Implementing the seven-step executive calling process				
Formulating indirect strategy				
Performing a business analysis				
Qualifying a major opportunity				
Qualifying a short cycle opportunity				

Are You a Selling Fox?

Do you want to be a Selling Fox? Are you willing to make the investment in your own development that it takes to become a Selling Fox? If the answer is *yes*, you will need to reevaluate everything that you are doing, addressing the following questions:

- How Fox-like are you now?
- Is your sales manager the right manager for you, in terms of optimizing your performance and development?
- Are you working for the right company with the right culture for you to develop into a Selling Fox?
- Are you selling the right types of products or services to maximize your success?
- Are you selling into the right territory?

Becoming a Selling Fox is creating a personal asset of the highest value. All of the more significant aspects of what you do in selling should be considered in that light. Do they advance your development or impede it? Let's examine each of the preceding questions:

🦊 How Fox-like are you now?

To answer this question, run the Selling Fox Evaluator, shown in Table 9.2, on yourself. The key here is not to be too critical of yourself, but to know where you are, which is the first step to improving.

If your score suggests that you are not yet a Selling Fox, and if you have not already done so, rate your self-performance using the tool shown in Table 9.1. In addition, run the Selling Fox Evaluator on yourself at least once per quarter and track your improvement. You may be surprised at how fast you develop.

The Right Manager

🦊 Is your sales manager the right manager for you, in terms of optimizing your performance and development?

The Peter Principle tells us that a person rises to the highest level of his or her incompetence. I believe in the corollary to that principle, that a person rises to the level of his or her manager's incompetence. If you are working for the wrong person, it will absolutely suboptimize your development and sales performance. Questions that will help you get a handle on this are:

Table 9.2 **Are *You* a Fox? The Selling Fox Evaluator**

Rate each item using the –2 to +2 values. Then total your answers and use the probable results at the bottom of the page to determine whether you are a Selling Fox.

Score	Definition
+2	I am confident this is true.
+1	This is most likely true.
0	I don't know.
–1	I doubt this is true.
–2	I am confident that this is not true.

Salesperson's Name:

Fox Evaluator Questions	Score
1. I have exerted influence outside of my defined organizational authority.	
2. I have knowledge of my company's mission and business goals, as evidenced in my working to directly or indirectly advance them.	
3. I am an effective risk taker, in terms of my ability to assess and manage risk.	
4. I demonstrate integrity, in terms of being unwilling to compromise my company or other individuals to advance my own aspirations.	
5. I am a good listener.	
6. I can appropriately and successfully work in exception to company policy.	
7. I influence important decisions before they are formally made.	
8. I have close relationships with others who possess expertise that I personally do not have, but that can be important to my success.	
9. I am not arrogant about my knowledge or sales performance, as evidenced by my willingness to help others, even to the extent of their receiving the credit for some of my accomplishments.	
10. I am diplomatic in how I operate, as evidenced by my rarely taking people on in a confrontational manner.	
Total your score	

Score	Results	
+14 to +20	You are a Selling Fox	
+7 to +13	You are an emerging Fox	
–20 to +6	You have potential—go for it!	

- Does your sales manager provide you with a codified or structured sales process that is optimized for your business?
- Does he or she clearly set expectations relative to your implementation of specific sales practices?
- Do you consistently receive helpful coaching support when you need it?
- Does your sales manager create recognition opportunities for you within your company, helping you to increase your personal currency?
- Does he or she assist you in quickly securing resources when necessary to support a competitive sales situation?
- Is your manager a Selling Fox?

Note: If you are a sales manager or director, can you answer *yes* to all of the above, as they relate to your sales reports?

The Right Company

 Are you working for the right company with the right culture?

We have talked about the values, or ethos, of a Fox. It doesn't take a rocket scientist to figure out that this type of individual cannot survive in certain company cultures, as their values and/or operating philosophy would conflict. If you have ever been asked to do something in an account that you knew was wrong, you know what I am talking about. You are suddenly put in a lose-lose position. Either you compromise yourself or possibly your customer, or you compromise your position in your company. It is a completely unacceptable situation. In some other companies, sales as a business function is not appreciated, or perhaps it is misunderstood. Here, at best, your good work can easily be discounted, and at the least, you can be viewed as expendable.

A Selling Fox does best in companies that are customer-centered and that personify certain central operating values, such as quality, integrity, and innovation.

If you look at a company's business practices and at its people, products, and services, and you see these values evident and at work, you are in the right place to develop the attributes of a Fox and achieve significant success.

The Right Products and Services

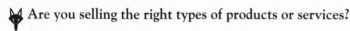

Are you selling the right types of products or services?

To develop the skills and knowledge that are necessary to become a Selling Fox, you need to be involved in the right type of selling. That is not to say that high levels of performance cannot be reached independent of what you are selling, but it does suggest that some forms of selling are more conducive to developing Fox-like skills than are others. The issue is one of *time*. In the type of selling that you do, is there sufficient time and opportunity to develop Fox-like skills and knowledge? If you are constantly pushing *product* and never allowed the time or opportunity to develop *solutions* for your customers, you may be successful in meeting quotas; but without the time and opportunity to expand your skill base and take on more diverse challenges, you may not become a Selling Fox. That is not to say that a Selling Fox could not be very successful in such an environment, but it is unlikely a person could *become* a Selling Fox in that self-limiting type of selling environment, in terms of developmental opportunity.

The Right Territory

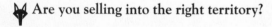

Are you selling into the right territory?

Just as larger ticket sales represent a good developing environment for Selling Foxes, the type of territory into which you sell is also a factor. Optimum is a small number of major accounts or an industry (vertical) market in which you can afford to build significant expertise in the customer's business. If you revisit the questions put forth in the Currency Tabulator (Table 5.3), you will see how a limited market focus enables you to develop better solutions for your customers. This is often a *team-selling environment,* which is highly conducive to developing Fox-like skills and knowledge. It can also be invaluable in developing a more visionary and business-oriented account and territory management process that is specific to you as a sales professional. This process is discussed in detail in Chapter 10.

The Fox Ethos

Adding to our list of Fox-like attributes as they relate to this chapter, we continue:

The Fox Ethos

Selling Foxes are very sensitive to their operating environment, seeking out companies that are customer-centered and oriented to quality, integrity, and innovation in their business practices.

Selling Foxes possess a very positive attitude toward self-development, welcoming feedback.

10

Building Your Personal Business Development System

Accelerating your personal development is key to becoming a Selling Fox, but equally important are two other advanced performance factors that all together, enable you to quickly reach your full sales potential. These additional factors consist of:

- *Building your personal selling philosophy*, such as the one that we have been cataloging throughout this book. The Selling Fox ethos is a source of wisdom that governs the actions and shapes the attitudes of a Selling Fox. Such high performers recognize that understanding the mechanics of selling, even with good interpersonal skills, is not enough to beat the competition and consistently exceed quota.
- *Building your personal business development (sales) system*, consisting of specific sales practices that will assist you in systematically driving the development of your sales territory and accounts.

The Missing System

The combination of a solid approach to personal development, combined with a strong ethos or selling philosophy and an effective business development system is very powerful, and yet it is something that generally is not very well understood.

In my first book, *Power Base Selling: Secrets of an Ivy League Street Fighter*, we introduced a selling methodology to assist you in waging a winning competitive sales campaign, focusing heavily on leveraging customer politics and formulating competitive strategy. Published in 1990 and still in print, *Power Base Selling* presented topics rarely addressed before; these topics have since become the basis for virtually every successful competitive selling methodology. Now, as the corporate landscape and the selling environment change kaleidoscopically, knowing sales process is still very important, but process alone is not enough to assure the success of a Selling Fox.

Later, in *World Class Selling: The Crossroads of Customer, Sales, Marketing, and Technology*, published in 1999, we focused on the *organizational* aspects of optimizing a company's business development efforts through the alignment of sales, marketing, human resources, and technology. This alignment or synchronization of company functions was based upon the buying patterns of a company's customers, further aligning the interests of supplier and customer. Thus, in those two books, we addressed the two ends of a continuum, with competitive sales methodology at one end and the company organizational structure needed to optimize sales at the other. What was lacking in the center of that continuum was a personal business development system for the sales professional, a system that can cover all the different sales opportunities that you, the active salesperson in the field, might pursue in order to make quota year after year. This book is intended to fill that center position.

Design an Effective System

In this final chapter, we take you through a system of proven sales practices, utilizing the concepts presented in earlier chapters, to model a personal business development system that you can adapt and tailor to your own selling environment. Master this system and combine it with a Fox-like selling philosophy, and you will have more control over your selling career and success than ever before. For a Selling Fox, an effective personal business development system is the key to self-determination.

Your personal business development system can be implemented individually or by a team, creating a strong infrastructure to support virtual teamwork. It will also take into account large customers and small ones, big-ticket sales and short-cycle opportunities, as it provides a holistic view toward sales opportunity management. Core to this view is account and territory planning. Let's look at why it is so important.

Begin with Account and Territory Planning

As a salesperson, your primary responsibility is to make quota successfully, developing excellent-to-good quality business in accordance with your sales forecasts and with the operating philosophy and policies of your company.

You also have to anticipate an increasing quota over time—and potentially, a decreasing territory or account base. This requires not only that you be focused on today's business, but also that you allot time and effort to building a pipeline for the future.

In car racing, there is a principle of *always staying ahead of the race car*. As you drive through the turns, you are constantly looking through the reference points and out ahead, knowing that the car will follow your eyes. If you don't, it can be a hair-raising experience. You will feel like you are holding on for dear life. You may be going fast, but it is scary, and unforgiving if you make a mistake.

Selling is much the same way. You may be winning deals, but what about next quarter and next year—are you prepared for the turns ahead? Although making a pit stop takes up valuable time that the driver hates to relinquish, it is necessary. Adding fuel, replacing tires, and fixing problems prepares the car and driver for the remaining laps, helping to ensure that the driver and his or her support team are able to perform to the maximum, working together in perfect cadence. This concerted effort will allow the driver and car to finish the race, hopefully in first place, well ahead of the nearest competitor.

Granted, account and territory planning takes time away from actual selling. However, that kind of planning will give you the same boost in performance that a pit stop does. It will keep you highly tuned and competitive. Account and territory planning will help you to identify early on from what direction new business will most probably come, along with what has to be done to pursue and secure that business. Think of it as a forward-viewing capability—*always staying ahead of your accounts*. With that knowledge, it will be easier to identify what resources may be required to get into or stay in competition for key business. It will also provide you with valuable insight as to where you should be focusing your time and efforts to make quota, not just this quarter, but for quarters into the future.

Account and territory planning, like racing or any other competitive endeavor, is a discipline that requires personal strength, innovation, self-confidence, and a strategic orientation, balanced by a street-fighter mentality. The salespeople who master it are almost always Selling Foxes, and for them this type of planning is core to their personal business development system, enabling them to

- Effectively manage multiple opportunities within an account or territory.
- Align the right resources with the right opportunities.
- Establish a common language that is meaningful and efficient.
- Bring leadership and strategic thinking to short-term and long-term sales efforts.

Applying Planning to Your System

The first requirement of any personal business development system is that it be highly *usable*. Systems that are overly simple are very usable but not sophisticated enough to be effective, while at the other end of the continuum, approaches that are all-encompassing become too time-consuming and difficult to use. The key is to strike a balance that maximizes both effectiveness and usability.

As we said earlier, your primary responsibility is to make quota, but to accomplish that, you need your personal business development system to assist you in three critical areas:

- Protecting and growing certain accounts that you cannot afford to lose
- Winning deals
- Creating new deals

Therefore, your personal business development system must accommodate the same types of accounts discussed in Chapter 7, where we introduced the Account Terrain Map (Table 7.1) and the Territorial Impact Business Map (Table 7.2). You'll recall that accounts fall into four categories:

- A—*Major accounts*, to be protected and grown, as they represent strong repeat business potential and/or are strategically significant from a referral or marketing point of view.
- B—*Competitive accounts*, in which short-term active and competitive sales situations exist.
- C—*Demand creation accounts*, in which you are developing the opportunity in a consultative manner, acting as a thought leader for the customer.
- D—*Maintenance and early development accounts*, in which you are maintaining a presence in accounts that are inactive or determining whether an account has the potential to become an A, B, or C account.

Generally speaking, all opportunities or accounts will fall into one of the aforementioned categories, whether it is a large multinational customer or a geographical territory. Your personal business development system will apply to both, as you can see from the following examples.

Application to a Global Account

Let's assume that you are responsible for a global account. There may be a corporate facility or division of the company that is very significant because of its size or influence on the rest of the organization—this itself would be considered a major account under the global account umbrella. Think of it as an account within an account. Other divisions might contain sales opportunities that are competitive. These are designated as competitive accounts, again under the global umbrella (Note: *All* sales situations, even those that represent repeat business, should be viewed as competitive. It is simply too easy for something like a customer reorganization, merger, shifting of internal priorities or key decision makers, or an unsuspected competitive thrust to seriously damage your competitive strength without warning).

Other accounts may not be in a buying mode now, but you see the potential to help the customer identify opportunities to enhance its business in the future—a benefit that will at the same time generate orders for you—these are demand creation accounts that reside under the global umbrella. Finally, some divisions may not represent any new business in the foreseeable future, but warrant a maintenance level of selling. These maintenance and early development accounts require care either because:

- You have an installed base within them.
- It enables you to maintain a presence, ready to move in the event that any meaningful changes occur within the accounts in the future.

The intent is to break down a large global account into a set of connected smaller accounts in order to produce enhanced manageability. We will do the same with a sales territory.

Application to a Geographical Territory

As we have discussed before, not all accounts are created equal. Some are more important than others, perhaps even essential to the development of a sales territory. These are the major accounts (*major* is a relative term, varying as sales territories vary, but typically it suggests an account that has significant future business development or sales potential and/or strategic value that warrants a sizable cost of sales investment).

At the same time, any territory will have a number of active sales situations going that need to be won. Again, we'll refer to these as competitive accounts within the territory. Just as in a global account, you will also have demand creation accounts, in which you are shaping future sales opportunities; last, you have maintenance and early development accounts that are more suspects than prospects.

Building Order Flow

When you think of order flow, don't think pipeline. Accounts, unlike sales opportunities, do not move on a one-way street from one phase of

Table 10.1 **Business Development Model**

Account Category		Goal
A—Major Accounts Focus: Protect & grow	⟶	Predictable sales flow
B—Competitive Accounts Focus: Win business	⟶	Shorter term, profitable orders
C—Demand Creation Accounts Focus: Create opportunities	⟶	Longer term, highly profitable orders
D—Maintenance & Early Development Accounts Focus: Build a presence	⟶	Provide future business

a pipeline to another. They move up and down; before we examine that phenomenon, however, let's look at the overall sales goals associated with each account category, illustrated in Table 10.1.

A one-way funnel or pipeline of opportunities operates solely at a deal level, typically moving sales from that of being suspects to prospects to qualified sales opportunities to the proposal phase of a sales cycle to the all-important closing phase. A personal business development system, on the other hand, accommodates the multidirectional movement of accounts, taking into consideration the following changes in account status:

- *A remains A*—A may grow larger and yet remain an A account.
- *A goes to B*—A's business may slow down, shifting its status to a B account.
- *A goes to D, then C*—A may be lost to a competitor, requiring that you shift into the D mode of rebuilding your support base. Over time, you may have the opportunity to transform it into a C account, quietly building your support base.
- *B remains B*—B may remain a B account: important, but not as significant as an A account.
- *B goes to A*—B may grow into an A account.

- *B goes to D, then C*—B may be lost to a competitor, causing you to regroup in the D mode, hopefully to then move into a C mode of sales coverage if the account has future sales potential.
- *C goes to B or A*—successful demand creation moves a C category account to a B or potentially to an A account.
- *D either drops out or goes to C, B, or A.*

These multidirectional movements represent the real world, in terms of what actually happens to accounts within a sales territory or global account. As such, it gives you the ability to

- Build an effective account or territory plan, ranking accounts according to their significance and the nature of the sales work required to develop them.
- Track the movement of accounts against your territory or account plan.
- Manage the account base, allocating the right resources to the right categories of accounts to support their development and maximum order flow.
- Expand the account base by specifically adding accounts to certain categories *at the right time* in order to keep your bookings flow steady and growing.

Assessing Your Personal Capacity

Let's apply this model to your own accounts, producing a profile of your present sales activities. First, answer the following questions and fill in the information in the chart provided in Figure 10.1.

- How many A accounts are there in your territory, or how many A divisions, if you are focused on a large global account?
- What percentage of your time is going into servicing these accounts or divisions?
- How many B accounts or active sales situations are you managing, and what percentage of your time is dedicated to that end?
- How many C accounts are you developing that will hopefully be-

Figure 10.1   **Account Profile Worksheet**

A Accounts		Time %	
B Accounts		Time %	
C Accounts		Time %	
D Accounts		Time %	
Dedicated to Internal Support		Time %	

come B or A accounts in the future, and again, what percentage of your time is going into this development process?

- How many early D accounts are you working on, and what percentage of your time is being invested to assess, move up, or move out these accounts?
- What percentage of your time is spent handling internal company support issues?

Now, take a look at the percentage of time dedicated to internal support versus time allocated to direct sales work. An optimum personal business development system requires that you spend no more than 25 percent of your work time on internal company or sales support issues, leaving 75 percent of your time to be devoted to direct sales work. If yours is skewed to higher percentages on the side of internal support matters, it is imperative that you take steps to get these percentages into proper balance, or your personal business development system will not operate effectively.

In terms of the number of accounts that a salesperson can effectively cover, there are no hard and fast rules, but a good starting point is a mix of two A, five B, five C, and anywhere from 5–25 D accounts. The numbers will vary depending on the type or nature of your selling efforts, ranging on a spectrum from a single large account to responsibility for a broad sales territory with many short-cycle sales opportunities. Recognizing where you fall on this spectrum is important to your finding the optimum mix of accounts that will maximize your business development efforts. With that insight, you will then be ready to plan your sales efforts for each of these A through D categories.

Evaluate Time Allocation for Focus and Balance

When you have identified the number of accounts and the percentage of your time dedicated to each category, you may find that you are allocating more than 100 percent of your available work time, and thus you are *overextended*, a condition often accompanied by a mix or focus problem.

If you are overextended, you will find it difficult to find time to do the necessary planning, even though the extra time devoted to that planning will improve the manageability of your accounts, thereby potentially increasing your sales hit rate and improving your personal capacity from a time standpoint. It is a difficult situation, just as it is in an enduro race when you cannot spare the time to make a pit stop; yet you know that if you don't do that, you probably will not make it to the end of the race.

At that point, timing becomes everything. Pit under the yellow flag and you will not lose position—a wonderful break. In selling, you need to find the yellow flag. To do this, list your accounts individually and identify what percentage of your time you are spending on each individual account. The key is to understand where you are underinvested or overinvested on a per-account basis. It is a balance issue, just as we have discussed when it comes to providing and receiving value. The same is true here: your investment in an account needs to be proportionate to the sales return.

You may also want to estimate how, within the near- to midterm, the numbers of accounts in each category might change, up or down. Look at how you can reallocate your work time to bring any over- and under-investments of time into better balance in order to accommodate your present and future account plans. Do this well, and it will be like "running under the yellow" with little negative effect on your selling efforts.

With a clearer, more objective understanding now of how much personal selling capacity you have and how that is being distributed based upon where and how you are allocating that capacity to sales efforts, you are ready to launch into building your own personal business development system. The next section takes you through the four components necessary to do that.

Build Your Personal Business Development System

Your personal business development system will consist of a mix of sales plans, each with its own purpose and structure (formally or informally), enabling you to protect and grow accounts, win deals, and create new sales opportunities.

The following four components make up the system, which you should modify or personalize to fit your own type of selling, accounts, and sales territory:

1. **Account team descriptions (including virtual teams) and account profiles** should be applied to A accounts.
2. **Winning sales plans** should be applied to all B accounts and A sales opportunities.
3. **Creating demand sales plans** should be applied to all A, B, and C accounts when appropriate.
4. **Relationship development sales plans** should be applied to all A accounts in which protection against competitive displacement is critical.

Account Team Descriptions and Account Profiles

Account team—this applies to an account that is large enough to require a dedicated or virtual sales and support team. In that case, who are the core and extended team members, and what are their respective roles in the account and their contact information?

Account profile—general information about the account:

Logistics—corporate and division locations and customer contacts

Organization chart—support base map

Business snapshot:

- Business definition
- Industry drivers
- Critical success factors
- Major challenges
- Critical business initiatives

Financial summary—to determine where the growth in their business has been and where the problem areas are; this is often based on a three-year review of the company's annual reports. This same type of analysis should be performed at the division or business unit level.

Marketing summary—to better understand the market segments the company serves, their products and services, and their percent market share; note whether their share in key market segments is growing, stable, or declining.

Competitive standing—to understand who the company's competition per-market segment is, how they are different, and competitive trends and threats.

Installed base—to identify equipment that you have installed within the account or services that you have provided; note who made the purchases, and when, generating what revenue for your company, and what results for the customer.

Identified sales opportunities:

- What to purchase
- Timing on the decision
- Revenue potential

- Buying criteria
- Your support base (strong, emerging, or weak)
- Competitors
- Sales strategy (direct, indirect, divisional, or containment)

Account revenue goal—take into consideration your personal hit rate in pursuing sales opportunities or the hit rate of the account team; determine your sales goal for the account, adjusted for hit rate. For example, assume that the revenue goal is $3 million for the current fiscal year, and that $1 million has been booked. Assume also that $800 thousand in new sales opportunities exist, and that your sales hit rate is 50 percent. As you can see in the following example, $1 million in sales has been closed, leaving $2 million to be generated for this account. Of that $2 million

- $800 thousand has been identified which, at a 50 percent hit rate, will actually produce $400 thousand in sales, leaving $1.6 million to be produced.
- At this same hit rate, producing $1.6 million in sales will require that you pursue $3.2 million in sales potential, as summarized here:

Revenue goal	$3,000,000
Year-to-date bookings	$1,000,000
Net goal	$2,000,000
Current opportunities	$800,000
Hit rate	50%
Current opportunities, adjusted for hit rate	$400,000
Adjusted net goal	$1,600,000
Sales potential goal	**$3,200,000**

What does this simple exercise in setting an account revenue goal tell us? To effectively develop an account or a sales territory, you need to know what you want and what will be required to get you there. In our example, we can conclude the following:

- You need to construct winning sales plans for pursuing the $800 thousand of potential business in order to maximize your hit rate, which can by no means be allowed to fall below 50 percent.

- You need to construct creating demand sales plans to develop the $3.2 million in sales potential. If your hit rate in pursuing the $800 thousand drops, you will need to identify and pursue a number higher than the $3.2 million. If your hit rate is higher than 50 percent, a smaller number will be required.
- If you are not able to identify $3.2 million in sales potential, you must achieve a higher hit rate through your winning sales plans.

A Selling Fox recognizes that the process of setting an account or territory revenue goal should be revisited every calendar quarter at a minimum, as an account or sales territory is a dynamic entity that does not lend itself to static goals.

A Selling Fox recognizes that hit rate is something that must be actively managed, as opposed to simply being a resultant measure of past sales performance.

Winning Sales Plans

1. *Create an opportunity profile*—an overview of the sales opportunity:

- Customer needs
- Customer contacts
- Sales objective; to sell what for how much by when
- Time frame
- Full description of the solution to be proposed

2. *Run the Major or Short Cycle Opportunity Evaluator*—this will identify missing information and determine whether you should be pursuing certain business and whether you can win (Tables 8.1–8.10).

3. *Build a value statement and launch the Calling High process*—the intent here is to begin constructing a strong support base as quickly as possible.

- Develop the insight necessary to begin building a more quantitative value proposition (Chapter 5).

- Implement the seven-step executive calling process (Chapter 5).
- Go Fox hunting—run the Fox Evaluator (Table 5.1).
- Identify his or her personal agenda (Chapter 5).
- Run the Contact and Competitive Contact Evaluators (Tables 5.2 and 5.4).
- Run the Currency Tabulator (Table 5.3).

4. *Define your existing support base and set sales objectives to strengthen your base of supporters*—set objectives that center on moving supporters to allies and nonsupporters to supporters, along with neutralizing opponents. (Figure 5.4)

5. *Formulate your strategy*—what will you count on to win:

- Determine whether you should implement a direct, indirect, divisional, or containment strategy, giving particular attention to possible deployment of the indirect approach.
- Perform a business analysis to determine whether it is feasible to undertake deinstalling a competitor (Chapter 7).

6. *Map out the major tactics to implementing your strategy*—set a timeline for each significant tactic and identify the necessary resources to support them.

7. *Initiate trapping*—anticipate the competition's response and begin trapping. Plan how you will create a virtual minefield for the competition (Chapters 3 and 7).

8. *Probe for customer objections*—don't wait for problems to surface. Anticipate what you can and use the trial close technique to uncover any other issues that might be lurking. Be sensitive to their origin, always going deep into the customer's underlying concerns. Pay attention to competitively induced objections (Chapters 1 and 2).

9. *Block, close, and be prepared for loss recovery*—as the sales situation approaches the point of peaking, be prepared to control the timing of the close using the blocking techniques that we discussed earlier. Close explicitly, jumping any objections, and have your loss recovery plan ready to go on a moment's notice (Chapters 3 and 4).

10. *Identify your 90-day action items*—these should consist of description of action, objective, completion date, and person responsible.

Creating Demand Sales Plans

1. *Industry trends*—identify the predominant industry or national trends that will most affect the account, and discover the impact these trends are having, or could have, on the account.

2. *Identify nonperforming divisions or business units if you are dealing with an A account*—look for customer products or services that are not producing revenue growth for the customer, or conversely, look for those that might be producing a disproportionate amount of revenue or profit but are underleveraged by the customer.

3. *Define the critical business issues affecting these business units*—determine whether you can have a direct or indirect impact on these issues as they relate to your business, products, and services.

4. *Develop your value statement*—conceptually, draw a line from your offerings or solution to the appropriate critical business issues and the impact that you believe you can have on those issues (Chapter 5).

5. *Identify key customer executives*—initiate the calling high process, utilizing the value statement that you have developed. Continue the process until you have sufficient executive sponsorship, as evidenced by a strong support base. Be certain to go Fox hunting early, using all the sales tools provided (Chapter 5).

6. *Draft a preliminary value proposition*—again, this will quantify your potential impact on the customer's business and assist you in building momentum in the account (Chapter 5).

7. *Map out the funding process*—as this is a new initiative in which you have created the demand for your solution, funding will not already be present. Take direction from the customer Fox you have identified as to how the funding might or should be allocated and how you can assist in this process. Remember to monitor the funding approval process throughout.

8. *Strive for a single-source purchase*—stay in the driver's seat by requesting that the purchase be made on a single-source basis. This will require that:

- You justify your request, presenting value from the customer's point of view in setting up a single-source buy.
- You appeal to a customer Fox, being certain that your request does not conflict with his or her personal agenda.

If this is not possible, be certain that you are heavily involved in the generation of the request for proposal (RFP) to ensure that it is written around your strengths—try hard to get it wired, so to speak.

9. *Close the business as quickly as possible*—if there is no driving mechanism to create a sense of urgency for the customer to close the deal quickly, then create one by working with the appropriate customer Fox. Time is not in your favor at this point in the type of sales cycle in which you must create demand. The worst loss that you can experience in selling is a situation in which you do all the demand creation work, only to have the competition come in during the eleventh hour of the sales cycle and snatch the business away from you!

Relationship Development Sales Plans

1. *Construct a support base inventory*—run the Fox Evaluator and the Contact and Competitive Contact Evaluators on a wide range of customer executives, middle managers, and operations personnel (Tables 5.1, 5.2, and 5.4).

2. *List all nonsupporters and opponents*—prioritize individuals in terms of which ones you feel are the best prospects for investing the time and effort to build or rebuild relationships. Generally, you will seek out the more powerful customer individuals who are in the Power Base. However, there are also people who can't do much to advance your account development efforts but who can do a lot to hurt you. This needs to be carefully considered when determining where and on whom you will put your primary focus in your relationship development sales plan.

3. *Identify roles, responsibilities, and personal agendas*—develop a clear understanding of what the high-priority people do and what drives them in terms of their personal agendas.

4. *Develop a preliminary value proposition*—these are nonrevenue goals that do not relate to selling anything. They may center on fixing a long-standing support problem within an account or on extending yourself and your company to assist an opponent or nonsupporter relative to a specific business project or challenge. Perhaps partnering another account with such an individual is feasible, keeping in mind the need to manage any risk of an opponent's or nonsupporter's poisoning the well, so to speak, within other accounts. Specifically, identify:

- The preliminary nonrevenue value proposition.
- Customer individual or owner of the values.
- Your objective—for example, to move an individual from an opponent to a supporter in six months. Progress is tracked by using the Contact Evaluator.

5. *Use the calling high methodology to initiate executive contact*—the intent here is to launch a collaborative process that will begin by jointly defining a nonrevenue value proposition with the appropriate customer executive.

6. *Build the tactical and resource plan to achieve the value proposition*—this is largely an internal planning exercise; however, it is not uncommon to involve the customer in the process to reinforce the collaboration effort. Remember that the intent is to create a more trust-based relationship with the customer executive in which the effort to provide value is the vehicle.

7. *Determine how the new relationship will be maintained over time*—this is often one of the most difficult but most important aspects of a relationship development sales plan. Periodic contact must be maintained, requiring that your marketing department be on its game when it comes to programs that reinforce and strengthen the user base for your products or services. User conferences and other company-sponsored events are very important to customer relationship management efforts.

8. *Identify your 90-day action items*—these should consist of description of action, objective, completion date, and person responsible.

The Mark of a Selling Fox

Wherever you find a Selling Fox, you will find a person who has inaugurated some form of personal business development system. Even as a new race car driver, I quickly recognized that the most professional and most successful drivers all drove by a personalized system of preparation and execution that brought structure and consistency to their racing. Others feel their way around the track and sometimes do pretty well, depending on their intuitive instincts. They are often good drivers, but rarely are they the top professionals in the business.

Selling Foxes leave less to chance because they are wise enough to recognize that although there are no guarantees in life, the odds favor those drivers who always know where the car should be on the track at all moments in time, moving from reference point to reference point. In competitive selling, your reference points are the numbered steps in the winning sales plan, the creating demand sales plan, and the relationship development sales plan.

Follow them, know where you should be on the selling track to developing business, and you will achieve the consistent performance that will make you a true Selling Fox.

The Selling Fox Ethos

This chapter completes our cataloging of Fox-like attributes:

The Selling Fox Ethos

Foxes always balance intuitive ability with structure and accountability.

Foxes recognize the dynamic aspect of their endeavors, never applying static or unusable processes in a changing environment.

Appendix

Portrait of a Selling Fox

The Fox ethos segments at the end of each of the preceding chapters, when taken together, present a list of the attributes or characteristics that define a Fox. Here, the list of characteristics is drawn together to paint a composite portrait of the ideal Selling Fox.

Nothing is beneath true Foxes, nor at too basic a level for them to address, whether it is consistently revisiting the basics of selling or examining how they treat people who are trying to be helpful in offering ideas or suggestions.

212

Selling Foxes always go with the more direct, harder style of closing, specifically asking for the customer's commitment. They do not shy away from difficulty.

Foxes always take an approach that projects confidence and professionalism while at the same time conveying sincerity.

Foxes are rarely argumentative and always proactive in their selling techniques.

Foxes are never egotistical or self-occupied. Selling Foxes put the spotlight on the customer, not themselves, products, or services—the customer is always center stage.

Foxes personify integrity. Absent any history, establishing integrity involves creating a tangible expression of your commitment. Foxes' integrity is always evident in their work, which accelerates relationship building.

Foxes are extremely competitive by nature. Selling Foxes continually hone and employ techniques in the areas of negotiating, blocking, and trapping that will create competitive advantage for them.

Foxes are never superficial or unprofessional. Selling Foxes do not resort to negative selling or superficial ruses to win. They use their competitive selling abilities to outmaneuver and outsell the competition.

Foxes know that to acknowledge the negative is to be prepared, and that to be prepared is to maximize control over their own destiny.

Foxes are so rehearsed and attuned that loss recovery is second nature.

Foxes never give up! Selling Foxes let the customer see their steadfast confidence in the quality of their solutions.

Foxes practice continual self-development. It is very important that you take ownership of your own development, seeking out people who can coach and support you.

Selling Foxes don't labor unproductively on the past.

Selling Foxes manage their ego; it does not manage them.

Foxes recognize other Foxes and are masters of the art of relationship management.

Foxes build support bases, knowing that whoever has the strongest support base usually wins.

Foxes are not egocentric and run silent most of the time, not seeking personal recognition or boasting about successes—he or she is interested only in results.

Foxes are good listeners. This is fairly easy for Selling Foxes, who focus not on themselves, but on others.

Foxes maintain high standards of personal integrity, and seek out and align with others of high integrity.

Foxes are mission driven, attaching a higher purpose to anything significant, knowing well how to hook the agenda of a customer Fox for mutual advantage.

Foxes rely on measurable results, knowing that if you can't measure it, you can't manage it.

Foxes focus on balance and value, taking the long-term view toward ensuring success.

Selling Foxes will recognize and sell to a customer Fox, independent of their apparent involvement, or even lack of involvement, in the buy decision.

Selling Foxes will look at every potential sales situation from bottom to top, side to side, and from every angle—thinking geometrically.

Selling Foxes work behind the scenes, gathering insight and support, launching competitive initiatives only at decisive moments.

Foxes think first and act second, always creating a plan using the de-installation process to ensure the successful displacement of a competitor.

Foxes are very proactive, anticipating the competition and laying traps that cause competitors to damage their own credibility.

Foxes like balance; Selling Foxes always evaluate risk (magnitude and manageability) versus reward.

Foxes are strategic; Selling Foxes know that even fast-paced, somewhat commodity-oriented selling requires strategy and analysis.

Foxes value time; Selling Foxes prioritize opportunities to optimize time and resources.

Selling Foxes are very sensitive to their operating environment, seeking out companies that are customer-centered and oriented to quality, integrity, and innovation in their business practices.

Selling Foxes possess a very positive attitude toward self-development, welcoming feedback.

Foxes always balance intuitive ability with structure and accountability.

Foxes recognize the dynamic aspect of their endeavors, never applying static or unusable processes in a changing environment.

Index

Page numbers in italics indicate tables and figures.

A

Accounts, 197, 198–200
  A (major), 197
  B (competitive), 197
  business development model, *199*
  C (demand creation), 197
  D (maintenance and early development),
    197
Airbus, 109–111
Anderson, Bob, 113–114
*Art of War, The: Ancient Military Strategy for
    Modern Business* (Sun Tzu), 102

B

Blocking, 35–41
  Fox ethos, 51
Boeing, 109–111
Business accounts. *See* Accounts
Business contacts. *See* Executive calling process

C

Calling high. *See* Executive calling
Cisco Systems, 112–114
Closing:
  defined, 6–7
  dynamics, 24–34
  Fox ethos, 22–23
  techniques, 1–24
    advertising, 19
    close condition requirements, 25–26 (*see
      also* Customer acquisition process)
    customer buying process (*see* Customer buy-
      ing process)
    customer commitment, 18–20
    customer needs (*see* Customer needs)
    customer objections (*see* Customer objec-
      tions)

customer referrals, 11–15
indirect strategy, 15–18
mastering the basics, 5–7
operative phrases (Selling Fox talk),
    22–23
process, nine-step, 21–22
trapping (*see* Trapping)
Competition, de-installing, 119–143
  account profiles, 128–129
  assessing territorial impact, 122–127
    account terrain map, *123*
    potential business impact, *126*
    territorial business impact map, *124*
  customer dissatisfaction with competition,
    134–135
  developing insight, 131–132
  executive calling process, 128 (*see also* Exec-
    utive calling process)
  Fox ethos, 34, 143
  loss recovery, 141–142
  penetration opportunity, 133
  penetration timing, 133–134
  political opportunity, 132
  pre-penetration checklist, 129–130
  pursuit, 120–128
  summary, 142
  trapping the competition, 136–140
  See also Qualifying opportunities
Competitive Contact Evaluator™, 96–97
Contact Evaluator™, 79, *80–81* (*see also*
    Competitive Contact Evaluator™)
Contacts. *See* Executive calling process
Containment selling, 16
Cost of sales, 123
Currency Tabulator™, 82–85
Customer acquisition process, 25–28
  ability, 27–28
  readiness, 26
  willingness, 27

Customer buying process:
  approval process, 26–28
  vs. close condition requirements, 26
  decision-making process, 26–28
  funding, 27–28
  managing, 28–29
Customer Fox, concept of, 1–2
Customer needs, 29–33
  ability, 33
  commitment, 31–33
    sample engagement plan, 32
  Fox ethos, 34
  understanding, 29–31
Customer objections:
  delivery and missing approver objections,
    16–18
  negotiating customer objections, 39–40
  pricing objection, 7–11
    key response techniques, 9–10

D
Direct selling, 16, 119–120
Divisional selling, 16, 119–120

E
Executive calling, 68–101, 185
  balanced value, 74–88
    personal, 76–88
      agenda, 82
      Contact Evaluator™, 79–82
      currency (see Personal currency)
      relationship support, 79, 81
      Fox ethos, 99
    business, 85–88
      value proposition template, 85
      value statement template, 85
  principles, 69–74
    characteristics of a Fox, 70–74
    Fox Evaluator™, 74, 75
    personal agenda, 73–74
    Power Base® (see Power Base®)
  process (see Executive calling process)
  Selling Fox perspective on, 98
  summary of, 184–185
Executive calling process, 88–98, 185
  defining support base objectives, 92–94
    building a support base map, 93
    competition's support base, 93–94

support base map, 94
  with key players, 95
  developing value propositions, 94–95
  executive preconditioning, 90
  initial executive meeting, 91–92
  making contact, 90–91
  preparing for contact, 89–90
  value acknowledgment executive meeting,
    95, 97–98

F
Fox ethos, 22–23, 34, 51, 67, 99, 118, 143,
    182, 192, 211, 212–215
Fox Evaluator™, 74, 75, 93
Fox hunting, 74–76

H
Hard close, 7
Hewlett-Packard Company, 115–118
Holden International, 221

I
Indirect selling. See Selling, indirect

L
Loss recovery, 53–58
  detection time vs. response time, 56
  Fox ethos, 67
  Fox-like approach, 143
  preparation, 53–54
  principles, 57–58
  process, 58
  timing and keeping control, 54–57
  "what-if" exercise, 53

M
Major opportunity evaluator, 145–146
  I: Can we add value?, 146–151
    business impact, 148–149
    customer involvement, 146–147
    driving mechanism, 147–148
    measurability, 149–151
  II: Should we pursue?, 151–159
    customer competence, 154–155
    funding, 154
    future value, 158–159
    geography/resourceable, 151–153
    profitability, 157–158

risk assessment, 156
time frame, 153–154
III: Can we compete?, 160–166
  customer history, 162–163
  philosophical alignment, 163–166
  solution compatibility, 161–162
IV: Are we aligned to win?, 166–174
  decision-making process leverage, 166, 168
  established momentum, 171–173
  executive sponsorship, 170–171
  political leverage, 168–170
prioritizing opportunities, *177*
summary results, 173–177

O

Opportunity evaluator. *See* Qualifying opportunities
Oracle Corporation, 115–118
Overly, Mike, 115–116

P

Penetration triad, 130–135, 136
Personal business development system, 193–211
  account profile, 200–206
    defined, 204–206
    account team, 204
  account and territory planning, 196–200
    geographical territory, 198
    global accounts, 197–198
    order flow, 198–200
  Fox ethos, 211
  personal capacity assessment, 200–203
  sales plans, 203–210
    demand, 208–209
    relationship development, 209–210
    winning, 206–207
Personal currency:
  Currency Tabulator™, 82–85
  executive level, 85
  middle management level, 85
  operations level, 85
Power Base®:
  defined, 1–2
  identifying, 73–76
Power Base Selling: Secrets of an Ivy League Street Fighter, 16, 194
Profit potential per account, 123–124

Q

Qualifying opportunities,144–182
  Fox ethos, 182
  major opportunity evaluator (*see* Major opportunity evaluator)
  short-cycle opportunity (*see* Short-cycle opportunity evaluator)
  summary of, 185–186

R

Rosser, Mike, 116–118

S

Sales examples:
  Airbus takes on Boeing, 109–111
  applying the indirect strategy, 130–131
  assessing territorial impact, 122–127
  building a support base map, 93–94
  Cisco: Taking on the competition, 112–114
  delivery and missing approver objections, 16–18
  early trial close, 24–25
  indirect strategy matrix, 103–107
  negotiating customer objections, 39–40
  Oracle takes the lead in CRM, 115–118
  pricing objection, 7–11
  self-performance rating evaluation, 63–65
  surprise negative referral, 11–15
  trapping to the competitive end run, 20–21
  trapping to negative selling, 41–43
  trapping to price discounting, 45–47
  trap snaps on negative selling, 43–44
  trap snaps on price discounting, 47–49
Sales hit rate, defined, 123
Self-assessment. *See* Selling, self-assessment in
Selling, indirect, 16, 100–118, 119–120, 185
  applying the indirect strategy, 130–131
  competition, de-installing, 119–143 (*see also* Competition, de-installing)
  by direct selling, 119–120
  by divisional selling, 119–120
  Fox ethos, 118
  Fox-like qualities, 107, *108*
  indirect strategy matrix, 103–107
  positive qualities, 102–103
  real-life examples, 109–118
    Airbus takes on Boeing, 109–111

Selling, indirect (*continued*)
  Cisco: Taking on the competition, 112–114
  Oracle takes the lead in CRM, 115–118
Selling, self-assessment in:
 achieving self-performance goals, 65–66
 Fox ethos, 67, 192
 ranking, 58–66
  difficult, 59, 183, 186, *187*
  hard, 59, 183, 186, *187*
  manageable, 59, 183, 186, *187*
  rating, 63–65, 183–192
   calling high, 184–185 (*see also* Executive calling)
   example self-performance rating chart, 64
   expanded self-performance rating chart, *187*
   indirect sales strategy, 185 (*see also* Selling, indirect)
   qualifying opportunities (*see* Qualifying opportunities)
   self-performance rating chart, 63
   self-performance rating evaluation, 63–65
   Selling Fox determination, 187–192
Selling Fox:
 concept of, 1–4
 Fox ethos, 192
 indirect nature of, *108*
 portrait of, 212–215 (*see also* Fox ethos)
 self-assessment, 183–192 (*see also* Selling, self-assessment in)
Selling Fox Evaluator, 188–189
Selling strategies:
 containment, 16
 direct, 16, 119–120
 divisional, 16, 119–120
 indirect, 16, 119–120 (*see also* Selling, indirect)
Selling techniques:
 advertising, 19

blocking, 35–41
customer objections, 38–41
customer presentation, 37
customer referrals, 11–15
first vs. last in, 35–37
Fox ethos, 51
negotiation, 40–41
trapping (*see* Trapping)
Short-cycle opportunity evaluator, 145, 177–82
Evaluator charts, *179–181*
Soft close, 6

T

Three-year sales potential per account, 123
Total category profit potential adjusted for hit rate over three years, 124
Total category sales potential adjusted for hit rate over three years, 124
Trapping, 41–50, 136–140
 defined, 19–20
 Fox ethos, 51, 143
 Fox outlook on, 49–50
 operative phrases (Selling Fox talk), 50
 price slashing (discounting), 45–47
 trapping to the competitive end run, 20–21
 trapping to negative selling, 41–43
 trapping to price discounting, 45–47
 trap snaps on negative selling, 43–44
 trap snaps on price discounting, 47–49
Trial close, 24–34
 defined, 7
 early trial close, 24–25

W

World Class Selling: The Crossroads of Customer, Sales, Marketing, and Technology, 16, 194

About the Author

Jim Holden is a pioneer in the development of competitive selling methodology for salespeople. As Chairman and CEO of Holden International, the largest independently owned business development firm specializing in sales performance solutions, he and his management team place heavy emphasis on the usability and effectiveness of their services. It is that same emphasis, as well as his desire to further the development of sales professionals by sharing the expertise he has gained during 30 years of successful selling, that have led to the creation of this field guide.

Underscoring the author's personal endeavors is a love of competition, the hallmark of a Selling Fox. When not involved in the business or with customers, he can often be found enjoying one of his favorite pursuits, racing his Ferrari 360 Challenge Car.

He and his wife Chris are also involved in programs designed to help break the cycle of homelessness in the city of Chicago and are equally

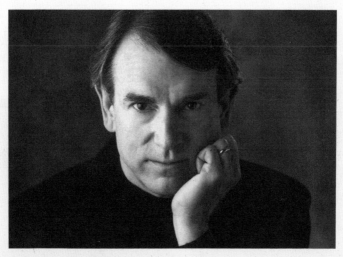

Author photo: Thomas Balsamo

supportive of their local church. Very fond of animals, they are active with the Brookfield Zoo, where Chris serves as a trustee.

Jim is no stranger to business readers, having published *Power Base Selling: Secrets of an Ivy League Street Fighter* and *World Class Selling: The Crossroads of Customer, Sales, Marketing, and Technology*, both published by John Wiley and Sons, and still in print.